Aron

Life on
Other Planets

Life on Other Planets

Emanuel Swedenborg

Translated by John Chadwick
Foreword by Raymond Moody

Swedenborg Foundation
West Chester, Pennsylvania

Swedenborg Society
London, England

© 2006, a co-publication of
The Swedenborg Foundation   and   The Swedenborg Society
320 N. Church Street   Swedenborg House
West Chester, Pennsylvania 19380   20-21 Bloomsbury Way
                                       London WC1A 2TH, England

Original title: *De Telluribus in Mundo nostro Solari, quae vocantur Planetae: et de Telluribus in Coelo astrifero: de illarum Incolis, tum de Spiritibus & Angelis ibi; ex Auditis et Visis*
First publication: London 1758.

The translation of this work, by John Chadwick, was originally published in 1997 by The Swedenborg Society (London) under the title The Worlds in Space. *No changes to the text, whether in spelling, wording, or punctuation, have been made.*

Cover image: NASA and The Hubble Heritage Team (AURA/STSCI); Image: STScI-PRC2004-10, "Light Echo" Illuminates Dust Around Supergiant Star, V838 Monocerotis (V838 Mon).

Library of Congress Cataloging-in-Publication Data

Swedenborg, Emanuel, 1688-1772.
    [De Telluribus de Mundo nostro Solari. English]
    Life on other planets / Emanuel Swedenborg ; translator, John Chadwick ; foreword by Raymond Moody.
        p. cm.
    Includes bibliographical references and index.
    ISBN: 0-87785-320-7
    ISBN-13: 978-0-87785-320-6
    1. Cosmology. I. Title.

BX8712.E3 2006
289'.4—dc22   2006011554

Design by Sans Serif, Inc., Saline, Michigan
Set in Galliard by Sans Serif, Inc.
Printed in the United States of America.

Contents

Are We Alone in the Universe?

In the twenty-first century, the search for intelligent, extra-terrestrial life is a respectable frontier discipline of science. The rapid advance of technical knowledge is making it increasingly likely that someday, perhaps soon, astronomers will answer one of the biggest questions of existence. Of course, it is impossible to predict exactly when that day will come. When it does, though, it will precipitate an unprecedented global shift in consciousness. Science, religion, and other central institutions of human society will be changed forever. Scholars of every discipline will rush to uncover what great thinkers of the past had to say about contact with rational inhabitants of other worlds. This quest will quickly lead them to the works of the finest polymath of modern times, Emanuel Swedenborg (1688–1772).

Swedenborg wrote perceptively, and presciently, about this subject in the eighteenth century. His works are full of fascinating insights that can contribute to this new burgeoning scientific enterprise. He foresaw possibilities that not even today's experts have imagined or addressed.

In the absence of definite information, any statement about extraterrestrial intelligence must be to some degree a personalization. So it is a great professional honor that the Swedenborg Foundation Publishers has allowed me to comment on *Life on Other Planets*.

This amazing work has enthralled me since the 1950s. I was a dedicated amateur astronomer from the age of eight. At that time, many professional astronomers believed that the sun was probably virtually unique in having a retinue of planets. They regarded planetary formation around a star as a fluke, an outlandishly improbably occurrence. These astronomers seriously entertained the notion that human beings might very well be the only sentient creatures in the universe. All this ran counter to my own heartfelt intuitions. Who was I, though, a mere youngster, to question eminent authorities?

Imagine my delight and surprise when, sometime around 1956, my father, himself a polymath, placed Swedenborg's little book about extraterrestrials in my hands. I distinctly remember the joy of first reading Swedenborg's opinion that "anyone of sound intellect can deduce from many facts known to him that there are many worlds and people living on them" (*Life on Other Planets* §3).[1] These were my sentiments exactly, and I suddenly felt a friend reaching out to me across two centuries.

Some years later, I entered the University of Virginia and became a philosophy major. I was intrigued by Plato's

---

1. As is customary in Swedenborgian studies, the numbers following titles refer to paragraph or section numbers, which are uniform in all editions, rather than to page numbers.

description of a near-death experience in *The Republic*. I began collecting accounts of the spiritual experiences of people who survived close calls with death. By 1974, I had interviewed more than one hundred individuals who told remarkably similar stories. They said that, when they almost died, they got out of their bodies and passed into a realm of light where they met loved ones who had previously died. They experienced a panoramic vision in which they saw their lives reviewed in exquisite detail. Then, when they were revived, they said they learned through their otherworld journey that the purpose of life is to advance in the capacity to love and to accumulate wisdom.

In 1974, when I was writing my book *Life After Life*, one of my professors of medicine mentioned Swedenborg's spiritual adventures. He said that Swedenborg's accounts bore many points of resemblance to the near-death experiences I had collected.

Frankly, it was some time before I realized, to my astonishment, that this was the same scholar whose work on extraterrestrials I had read as a child. So, although I am not a trained Swedenborgian, I have been grappling with his ideas in these two distinct contexts for about fifty years. I hope, then, that I will not be overstepping the mark in offering a personal opinion: namely, it is time someone does justice to Swedenborg's pioneering insights concerning the possibility of communicating with the sentient inhabitants of remote worlds in outer space.

This introduction approaches the task in four steps. The first section outlines recent breakthroughs in astronomy and biology that place Swedenborg's work in a new light. The second section comments on the reception Swedenborgians themselves generally accorded his work on extraterrestrial intelligence. The third section surveys eight major principles Swedenborg put forward in *Life on Other Planets* and shows their relevance to the current scientific debates. Finally, the fourth section sets his ideas about extraterrestrials in their historical context and compares them to those of other influential thinkers of his era.

I. Astronomy, Biology, and Intelligent Life in the Universe

Immanuel Kant (1724–1804) is generally credited with launching sidereal astronomy—the study of the realm of stars and galaxies—in 1755. By then it was realized that the fixed stars are suns like our own which appear small only because they are at enormous distances from the earth. Kant formulated three main ideas pertaining to the interstellar reaches. First, he stated that the Milky Way, which was an unfathomable mystery to the ancients, was an optical effect created by the diffuse light of myriads of stars too far away to be seen as discrete points. Second, Kant hypothesized that these stars were arranged into a gigantic disk that we now know as the Milky Way galaxy. Third, Kant conjectured that the nebulae, hazy patches of light seen in the heavens through the then-existing telescopes, were other incredibly distant galaxies of stars, comparable to our own Milky Way.

These three propositions revolutionized humankind's conception of the universe. Obviously, they were truly vast in their implications. Yet they were not fully agreed to by all astronomers until the early decades of the twentieth century.

There is some debate whether Swedenborg's *Principia*

Rerum Naturalium (1734) presages the disk theory of the Milky Way and the hypothesis that the nebulae are other galaxies. My own reading of the passages at issue inclines me to believe that he was indeed struggling with emerging notions that Kant formalized in 1755. After all, there is a tendency in the history of thought whereby revolutionary ideas are first set out in a preliminary and tenuous form and then later formulated clearly and more rigorously. At any rate, it is plain that ideas analogous to Kant's were percolating in Swedenborg's mind as early as 1734.

Until about 1990, it was entirely a matter of opinion and guesswork whether planets circled other stars. Even in the 1950s, some astronomers suggested that the planets of our solar system condensed from gas torn from the sun by gravitational field of another star that passed nearby eons ago. If so, planetary formation would be an exceedingly rare event, since near-collisions between stars are extremely unlikely. Either way, in the 1950s, it was generally agreed that human beings were destined never to find out. At that time, it was inconceivable that planets orbiting other stars could ever be detected from Earth. The distances were simply too great and planets simply too small relative to stars for direct observation of such bodies to be possible. As Swedenborg himself said of planets circling distant stars, "These are invisible to our eyes because of their immense distance, and because they shine only with light reflected from their own star, which again cannot reach us here" (*Life on Other Planets* §126).

Late in the twentieth century, however, enormous technological strides changed the picture dramatically. A revolution in the design and construction of telescopes, including orbiting telescopes such as the Hubble, turned what was once a pipe dream into practical reality;

consequently, as of mid-2005, astronomers have detected more than 150 exoplanets, that is, planets orbiting other stars. As would be expected, the first such bodies to be found were colossal, larger even than Jupiter. They were detected at first by measuring minute wobbles they induced in their parent stars as they spun around in their orbits. Then, soon, the technology was improving by leaps and bounds, and progressively smaller exoplanets were discovered. In March 2005, a sophisticated satellite, the Spitzer orbiting telescope, captured actual light emanating from two exoplanets. Shortly thereafter, on April 5, 2005, *The New York Times* science section featured the first photograph ever taken of a planet in another solar system. An article accompanying the photograph said, "The new planet will take its place as another landmark in an accelerating cavalcade of discoveries that have left astronomers fumbling for synonyms for 'historic'" (D4).

As I write, the race is on to find the first Earth-sized planets circling other stars. When that occurs, it will also be possible, by spectroscopy, to determine the chemical make-up of their atmospheres. In short, science has now fully confirmed what Swedenborg asserted two-and-half centuries ago. Planets circle most stars, perhaps nearly all stars.

Concurrently, developments in the science of biology have made it appear far more likely that life exists elsewhere in the universe. Formerly, scientists held that life could exist only under a quite narrow range of conditions. Hence, they did not bother to search for life in environments on earth where it was deemed to be impossible. Within the past few decades, however, exotic organisms have been found flourishing everywhere from scalding hot salt springs to frigid Antarctic wastes. Life has been found in extremely acidic waters, in radioactive pools around nuclear reactors, and in rocks retrieved from miles underground. It has shown up on the ocean floor around high-pressure volcanic vents. Life has proven a lot hardier than anyone believed until a couple of decades ago. Space scientists are currently evaluating the anomalous presence of methane on Mars, perhaps indicating the persistence of life on that planet. The case for extraterrestrial life is growing stronger with each passing month.

II. Extraterrestrials and the New Church

Apparently, *Life on Other Planets* has been a sticking point for some Swedenborgians. They accept his experiences of interacting with spirits of the deceased. However, they are uncomfortable with his accounts of conversing with the spirits of inhabitants of other planets. In 1897, in *The New Church Review*, Theodore F. Wright worried that "much ridicule has been heaped upon the New Church because its members believe the other planets to be intended, like this globe, for human habitation. Perhaps there is no point to which our people are so sensitive as this, for they continually hear scornful remarks, as if the single fact of our holding this belief were enough to discredit all else."[2]

I first lectured to Swedenborgian groups in the 1970s and 1980s. It was somewhat unsettling that, at that time, many people to whom I mentioned *Life on Other Planets* seemed somewhat embarrassed by it. To me the book seemed a sterling example of Swedenborg's prescience and

2. Theodore F. Wright, "The Planets Inhabited," *The New Church Review* 4 (1897): 117.

certainly a groundbreaking work in its own right. In the intervening years, however, the basis of their sensitivity has become more apparent. Sadly, much popular speculation about extraterrestrial life is thoroughly disreputable, a domain of flimsy pseudo-science, sensationalist journalism, conspiracy theories, flying-saucer religious cults, and wild tales of abductions by aliens. It would indeed be a travesty to see Swedenborg's work falsely equated with dubious claims and bizarre movements like those.

The ongoing scientific search for extraterrestrial intelligence is an entirely different matter, however. It is necessary to draw a sharp distinction between tabloid sensationalism and legitimate scientific investigation. Current research employs huge radio telescopes that scan the heavens in an attempt to pick up electromagnetic signals emitted by extraterrestrial civilizations. Scientists working on these projects hypothesize that they might intercept messages from the electronic devices by which members of an alien civilization communicate among themselves. Or some distant civilizations might be broadcasting information to make their presence known to sentient creatures in other parts of the universe. If so, scientists anticipate that those transmissions would contain mathematical constants presumably recognizable to rational beings throughout the cosmos.

This effort began in 1960 and has proceeded fairly constantly since then. In recent years, computers wedded to radio telescopes greatly increased the efficiency of the search. It is now possible to extract far more information from a single sweep of a radio telescope's antenna. Even with such advances, though, the process is slow and laborious. Thus far, only a minute portion of the sky has been scanned.

An array of planet-finding satellites scheduled for launch beginning in 2007 will significantly alleviate this problem. They will search for Earth-like planets in other solar systems. High-powered telescopes aboard these satellites should make the discs of such planets visible. Soon we will have photographs showing major geological features of Earth-sized bodies circling other suns. By spectroscopic analysis, we will learn their atmospheric composition and perhaps even detect the chemical signatures of extraterrestrial life. This data will enable radio astronomers to zero in on likely sites for extraterrestrial civilizations.

It sounds like science fiction, but it is science fact, and all who desire to do so can confirm it for themselves by consulting reputable science journals. Advances are taking place so rapidly that, as soon as they appear in print, they are superseded by even more incredible scientific revelations. New extrasolar planets are currently being discovered at the rate of about three per month.

It is in the context of this remarkable and potentially explosive expansion of knowledge that Swedenborg's writing on extraterrestrials takes on a new complexion. In short, there is absolutely nothing for Swedenborgians to be embarrassed about in *Life on Other Planets*. I contend that what Swedenborg said in that volume contributes to the current debate about extraterrestrials in at least three important ways.

First, it suggests possibilities for investigation that today's researchers have not yet considered. Second, it suggests novel ways of applying the knowledge that would be gained from the discovery of sentient extraterrestrial beings. Third, it makes principled, theological responses possible should intelligent life be found in outer space.

In the latter regard, in recent public debates about the

question of life on other worlds, representatives of some Christian denominations appear to be hiding their heads in the sand. They respond to queries on the subject simply by denying that life exists beyond earth. They assert, without any apparent rational justification, that the Bible absolutely rules it out. Yet, finding life elsewhere in the universe would be a singular transformation and a significant turning point in history. Therefore, it is prudent for theologians to be prepared for the possibility. Swedenborgian religious scholars would be in a uniquely privileged position to address the theological issues that the discovery would inevitably raise.

The next section clarifies and strengthens the above statements by surveying *Life on Other Planets*.

III. Swedenborg's Insights concerning Sentient Extraterrestrials

Life on Other Planets is perhaps the most controversial of Swedenborg's works, and it ought to be approached with a great deal of caution and self-awareness. It is conceivable that its full significance will not become apparent until more complete knowledge about extraterrestrial intelligence becomes available. Let me say in particular that I am not aiming for any sort of comprehensive interpretation or final, exhaustive statement on this extremely complex and thought-provoking document. Instead, I will sum up some insights on the work gained from several decades of personal study and reflection.

Much has been made of the fact that Swedenborg mentions certain worlds within our solar system: Mercury,

Jupiter, Mars, Saturn, Venus, and the moon. It is not useful, however, to identify them with the heavenly bodies we know by those names. Critics typically point out that Swedenborg's descriptions do not coincide with current astronomical knowledge relating to those worlds. Therefore, these critics contend, his visions were simply mistaken, and his book on other inhabited worlds can be dismissed out of hand.

Undeniably, this sort of criticism is appealing to those whose thought processes are primarily concrete and geared to the concerns of mundane reality. The trouble is that it is beside the point when addressing a work such as *Life on Other Planets* for three main reasons. In the first place, Swedenborg himself talks throughout the book of the profound difficulties of putting experiences like his into ordinary language. He also mentions that he could not decipher the communications of some of the beings he encountered and that some of what was passing between them was ineffable. Furthermore, he says, "in the spiritual world inhabited planets are not spatially remote as in the natural world" (*Life on Other Planets* §135). That is, the realms Swedenborg visited were not in the space-time continuum as we know it nor are the categories of earthly languages directly applicable to those realms.

Second, Swedenborg wrote at a time when certain symbolic associations still attached to the names of the planets. People still held onto old astrological associations and associations drawn from the humoral medicine of Galen. It would be unreasonable to read Swedenborg's narratives of his journeys beyond the Earth without taking their symbolic dimension into account. As a man of his era, he cannot be expected to have set ancient astrological and medical contexts completely aside in favor of a twenty-first century perspective that did not even exist when he was alive.

Third, literalistic criticism of Swedenborg's claims about extraterrestrials blinds the critics to the fascinating theoretical sweep of the book. In my opinion, these critics put the focus in the wrong place. I find much that is valuable here, which they miss because of rash attempts at debunking. Let me illustrate this by discussing eight major points Swedenborg makes in *Life on Other Planets*.

1. It takes someone with a severely constricted mind to jump to the conclusion that we are alone in the universe.

This was true when Swedenborg said it, and it is even more clearly so today. Swedenborg felt certain that unseen planets accompanied distant stars, but that was not an item of established knowledge in his lifetime. It is established beyond question, however, in the twenty-first century.

So it takes a kind of failure of the imagination, and perhaps a degree of fear as well, to cling to the conviction that we earthlings are the only intelligent creatures in the cosmos. After all, facing up to the existence of extraterrestrials will require a complete remodeling of familiar systems of thought. It may involve abandoning fundamental presuppositions that many people cherish and regard as absolute. So, for some, accommodating oneself to the reality of life beyond this planet will be a painful and even frightening process. No one who has studied Swedenborg doubts that he was an immensely courageous man and one who was comfortable setting timeworn assumptions aside if they stood in the way of his pursuit of truth. In this regard, there is much more to his work than the enlightenment we can find in his specific statements about extraterrestrials. We can also find in his character a model for how to respond when clear and convincing proof of extraterrestrial intelligence finally comes to light. It is becoming increasingly evident that there must be an innumerable multitude of inhabited worlds. Yet only a few towering figures in the history of thought have been able to transcend a sort of mental terracentrism. Plainly, Swedenborg was one of them.

2. Spirits of the deceased from every inhabited planet congregate around that planet and serve the sentient beings who live there.

Now, unquestionably, this is a radical assertion that is monumental and even staggering in its import. Swedenborg says that the afterworld comprises more than just the spirits of the departed that come from our own planet. It also includes the spirits of the departed that come from other worlds throughout the universe. How are we to react to such a far-reaching and portentous statement?

Again, it takes a certain failure of imagination, and a certain fearfulness, to shrink from the implications of Swedenborg's bold proclamation. Suppose we grant that there must be sentient, living entities elsewhere: by what right could we deny them a continuation of consciousness beyond death? Ultimately, many more difficulties would arise from denying Swedenborg's position than from tentatively agreeing to it. To deny it would enmesh the one who denies the premise in many untenable *ex post facto* rationalizations. It would also betray a kind of arrogance and self-centeredness. Assume that there must be thinking, feeling beings on other worlds in outer space. Assume also that we human beings live on after death. Granted both assumptions, there could be no evident, rational basis for denying that extraterrestrials might survive death too.

It cannot be denied that, on first hearing, Swedenborg's pronouncement is startling and even seems wildly implausible. Yet, upon reflection, one sees that it would be even more wildly implausible for it not to be true. What remains—the strong resistance that many will doubtless feel toward Swedenborg's proposition—is a purely psychological one, not a logical or rational consideration. Besides it is already abundantly clear that many people will find it psychologically extremely difficult to adapt to the presences of other intelligences in our universe. So we ought to be grateful to Swedenborg for grabbing the bull by the horns, as it were, and confronting this issue courageously. Humanity will have to face it collectively one day; at least, that is how it now appears, based on the best available astronomical and biological knowledge.

Incidentally, a few people who told me of their near-death experiences related details that correspond exactly to Swedenborg's position. Invariably these were individuals whose cardiac arrests went on for so long that there is no medical accounting for their having survived. Yet survive they did, and their near-death experiences were among the most profound anyone related to me. They said that, when they went into the next life, they became aware that the after-death world literally embraced the cosmos. They experienced Earth as only one remote outpost of a vibrant, spiritual reality that also comprehends spirits from worlds far beyond our own. None of these subjects ever communicated directly with the denizens of other worlds. However, they sensed by some means they could not put into words that such beings definitely exist. My subjects also said they were given to know that otherworld spirits are mentally and spiritually accessible to those on the other side.

Swedenborg's insistence that the afterworld includes spirits from other planets certainly makes life after death a more exciting prospect. It is encouraging, in that regard, that some individuals with profound near-death experiences say essentially the same thing. If they are right, the world beyond death is bound to be a wonderful place for those who love learning.

3. Spirits in the afterlife continue to learn and are continually increasing in wisdom.

Here, too, Swedenborg's discoveries are in line with what people with near-death experiences report. Dr. George Ritchie, for example, was the first person I heard describe a personal near-death experience. I first heard him discuss his experience in 1965. I can say without hesitation that he remains the finest man I have ever known. His experience, which he narrates in his book *Ordered to Return*, took place in 1943. He states that, during his prolonged cardiac arrest, he became aware of an entire parallel dimension of reality, which he compared to an institution of higher learning. He is confident that, as he puts it, learning does not stop when we die but is "a process, I gather, that goes on for eternity."[3]

I have heard similar accounts from about a dozen other survivors of close calls with death. Again, these were individuals who had incredibly lengthy cardiac arrests and

---

3. George Ritchie, *Ordered to Return: My Life After Dying* (1943; rpt. Charlottesville, Va.: Hampton Roads Press, 1998).

particularly deep, profound near-death experiences. They are in complete agreement with what Swedenborg asserts, namely, that an educational process continues after bodily death. In his account, the world beyond death is an inexhaustible repository of knowledge from worlds throughout the universe. There even seem to be spirits who can leave our solar system and travel to other solar systems to acquire knowledge relating to the planets there.

4. The intelligent inhabitants of other worlds differ from us in their physical bodies, emotional makeup, and cognitive capacities.

Science fiction movies often portray aliens as looking quite unlike human beings. In this respect, Swedenborg's picture of extraterrestrials does not correspond to the popular image. His extraterrestrials are more like us than unlike us. There are some differences, of course. For example, during his visit to a planet beyond our solar system, he sees men "with faces the colour of human flesh, as in our world. But there was a difference; the lower part of their faces was black instead of bearded, and their noses had a whiter colour than flesh" (*Life on Other Planets* §162). Overall, however, Swedenborg describes the intelligent inhabitants of other planets as closely resembling humans on Earth in their essential bodily configurations.

However much this may diverge from popular conceptions, it corresponds to what some exobiologists—scientists whose research centers on the possibilities of extraterrestrial life—expect on independent grounds. These exobiologists reason that the humanoid configuration is an efficient design for intelligent life and that evolutionary pressures might well reproduce it elsewhere in the universe. At present, though, the determination of this issue is beyond the reach of science. For now, it seems wise to register Swedenborg's observation and wait patiently for the eventual outcome.

Swedenborg's extraterrestrials often differ markedly from earthlings in their emotional qualities. In comparison with us, for example, the inhabitants of Jupiter are exceptionally gentle and sweet. However, Swedenborg focuses primarily on cognitive differences between the humans of our Earth and intelligent entities from distant planets. For example, the spirits of Mercury are notable for their memory but "are not particularly distinguished for their powers of judgment. They take no pleasure in matters requiring judgment or in inferences from known facts. It is the bare facts that give them pleasure" (§17). Jovians, on the other hand, "define wisdom as good and fair thinking about the events which happen in the course of living. . . . They neither know nor wish to know anything about the sciences we have in our world" (§62).

Today's scientific investigators would do well to consider what Swedenborg had to say. His observations and comments concerning cognitive differences among various kinds of extraterrestrials present interesting potential difficulties for current research assumptions. The present-day scientific search presupposes that aliens proceed, as we do, by the scientific method. However, Swedenborg remarks that the inhabitants of some planets lack science as we know it. That would greatly complicate the problem of communicating with them, at least by the methods that scientists are now contemplating. This insight should be an impetus to think in more depth about how we might reasonably expect basic concepts of knowledge itself to vary among different species of intelligent creatures. Indeed, a notion of a kind of comparative epistemology is implicit in Swedenborg's approach. It is an exciting thought that someday we may gain entirely new perspectives in our own concepts of knowledge by comparing them to concepts arrived at independently by rational beings from other worlds. If that happens, Swedenborg will have pioneered a mode of rational inquiry unimaginably vast in its implications for humanity.

Swedenborg conversed with sentient entities from other worlds when he was in a profound, altered state of consciousness. Yet today's models contemplate transactions with extraterrestrials taking place between Earth's scientists and scientists from alien worlds, as it were. That picture implies that participants on both sides would be in the analytical, ego-aware state of awareness associated with scientific investigation. However, Swedenborg's encounters suggest that might not be the only way to communicate with extraterrestrials or even the best way. Altered states of consciousness such as mystical awareness or the hypnagogic state might serve the purpose better. At any rate, an event of the magnitude of encountering an intelligent entity from another world could reasonably be expected to induce an altered state of consciousness. The mind would go into high gear as it attempted to come to terms with an occurrence so far beyond all previous human experience. Here again, musing on Swedenborg's work brings fascinating possibilities into view that stand to enrich existing research methodologies.

5. *Truth is a universal value.*

In the past, on Earth, contact between widely different cultural and ethnic groups has bred cultural and ethical

relativism. Moreover, a sort of relativism about truth itself
became fashionable in the twentieth century and persists
into the twenty-first. People say, almost as a mantra,
"What's true to me is true to me, and what's true to you is
true to you."

How easy it is to forget that truth is, by definition, that
which is the case independently of what any individual may
believe, perceive, or imagine. Ultimately, the doctrine that
truth is a matter of individual opinion is an outright self-
contradiction. Swedenborg emphasizes that truth holds
throughout the universe, as a standard that is common to
us and to the inhabitants of other planets. There is a moral
component to truth, too, as he recognizes. He reminds us
that "all mental activities, that is, activities of thought and
will, relate to truth and good" (§163). As humankind
stands on the threshold of encountering extraterrestrial intelligence, that is good advice to keep in mind.

6. Intelligent entities from other worlds can commu-nicate via symbols.

In conversing with the spirits of a planet in another solar
system, Swedenborg compared them to eagles. He was al-
luding to their keenness of vision, but the spirits took of-
fence. They thought he was implying that they were
predatory, like an eagle. To straighten out the situation, he
had to explain his metaphor to them (*Life on Other Planets*
§140).

During his sojourn with the spirits of Jupiter, he noted
that the inhabitants of that planet have an innate fear of
horses. He explained their fear in terms of the spiritual
sense of *horse*, which "means the intellectual faculty formed
from factual knowledge" (§60). The Jovians are afraid of

the intellectual faculty with its propensity to worldly sciences. Hence, that fear transfers to horses, the symbolic equivalent of the sciences. Accordingly, they experience an influx of fear when they think of horses because of the connection with intellectual knowledge (§60). Both of the above incidents and others as well indicate that rational beings in different parts of the universe share a common faculty of symbolic thought and expression.

This is a more nuanced view of the possibilities of communicating with extraterrestrials than is present in many of the current scientific discussions. The latter contemplate primarily the transmission of purely scientific concepts and information between earthlings and extraterrestrials. The underlying assumption seems to be that communication will be through the medium of logic as we know it, which is predicated on literal language. Swedenborg's work prompts us to consider also the possibilities of a symbolic mode of communication that transcends the merely literal.

On Earth, human beings have been shaped by the use of symbols. In fact, symbolic thought and behavior are part of what it means to be a human being. No other species engages in symbolic behavior remotely comparable to that which human beings have evolved. Since, therefore, it is part of what defines us as human, it stands to reason that the capacity for symbolism is one of the criteria by which we would recognize an entity from another world as sentient and intelligent.

Contact with intelligent beings from outer space is sure to provoke a thorough rethinking of the entire concept of communication. Scholars will need to reconsider the most basic concepts of linguistics. When they get to that juncture, they will find that Swedenborg covered some of the same territory in *Life on Other Planets*.

7. A spiritual bond exists between the human beings living on Earth and sentient, intelligent beings inhabiting other worlds throughout the universe.

What is the nature of the relationship between conscious, rational denizens of distant planets and human beings? It seems likely that twenty-first-century science will propel that question to the forefront of humankind's intellectual, academic, moral, spiritual, and religious agendas. The day is drawing ever closer when we will encounter our counterparts from other worlds. When we establish contact, how will we relate to them? How will they relate to us? Is there anything in history that could guide us through such portentous and unprecedented developments?

In the twentieth century, poplar science fiction movies portrayed extraterrestrials as our mortal adversaries. Let us hope that the specter of interplanetary warfare remains forever confined to the realm of fantasy. Other popular movies and books of that era, as well as a few bizarre religious cults, viewed extraterrestrials as our saviors, bringing salvation from outer space. That image demeans humanity, however, and could appeal only to those with diminished self-esteem.

On the other hand, astronomers who lead the serious scientific search for alien intelligence hope to commune with their fellow scientists from other worlds. The work these scientists are conducting is of immense potential significance for all humanity. We should praise them highly and commend them for their pioneering research. We should congratulate them for the mountains of sensational new knowledge they have so rapidly accumulated.

I believe we should also forgive them for the strong undercurrent of scientism that runs through their work. After all, it is perfectly understandable that many scientists would subscribe, even if only unconsciously, to scientism, the doctrine that the scientific method is the only way to find out the truth and establish knowledge. The tremendous, highly visible accomplishments of science during the past two centuries seem to lend credence to scientism. Progress in the humanities certainly seems to pale in comparison.

Even so, if one thinks the doctrine of scientism through carefully, it collapses under its own weight. To see this, suppose one were to ask proponents of the doctrine how they know scientism itself is true. Answering that they know from the scientific method would be circular reasoning (the fallacy of *petitio principii*), whereas answering that they know from philosophy, history, literary theory, theology, the law, or any other learned discipline would contradict the premise of scientism.

It is practically a certainty that the initial discovery of extraterrestrial intelligence will come from science. When that happens, however, it will electrify scholars of every field, and they will instantly become involved in interpreting the discovery. Making sense of a revelation of that magnitude will require scientists, surely. Just as surely, it will also require philosophers, logicians, linguists, historians, sociologists, psychiatrists, and theologians. It may even require entire new learned disciplines that we cannot yet imagine or foresee.

The doctrine of scientism is not a useful principle for thinking about extraterrestrial intelligence. Swedenborg was a seasoned, insightful scientist, but he never succumbed to scientism. It must be emphasized that he conceptualized our relationship to the sentient inhabitants of other planets as a spiritual one—that is, we share with them a spiritual nature and a connection through one, universal, loving God.

8. There is only one God for the entire universe.

The above proposition is the core belief that defines monotheism in general. In most monotheistic religious systems, however, the role of God seems strangely constricted. He is occupied exclusively with the moral governance of the human beings who live on this one small planet. That leaves the purpose of an unfathomably immense swath of the universe unaccounted for. Terracentric monotheism remains silent on the status of trillions of other planets. What is their place in the scheme of things?

I will leave theology to the theologians. To me, however, it seems a virtue of Swedenborg's thought that he peopled those innumerable worlds with sentient beings who share a spiritual bond, through one God, with humans who live on Earth. It seems consistent with the infinite glory and love of God that he would reveal himself in the lives of extraterrestrials too. It is an altogether more uplifting view of God, in my humble opinion. It is also one that seems in harmony with the astounding astronomical and biological knowledge of the twenty-first century.

IV. The Historical Context of Swedenborg's *Life on Other Planets*

In the eighteenth century, lines of demarcation among astronomy, philosophy, and religion were not drawn as sharply as they are today. The great thinkers who were then formulating what evolved into modern cosmology were as much spiritual visionaries as they were scientists. Integrating the physical world into the spiritual realm was a central concern of their budding cosmological theories. Through these men's works, the notion of extraterrestrial intelligence was rapidly becoming conventional wisdom. Eminent scholars felt certain that sentient creatures inhabited other planets in our solar system and planets in the solar systems of other stars. In that intellectual environment, Swedenborg was much a man of his time. However, the grounds upon which he espoused extraterrestrials set him apart from other contemporary thinkers.

His contemporaries supported their advocacy of sentient extraterrestrials by two main lines of reasoning. First they argued by analogy. Since the other planets that circle the sun resemble Earth in so many other respects, they must also be like Earth in being inhabited. Similarly, distant stars are like the sun, so they, like the sun, must be accompanied by their own inhabited planets.

The second type of argument these men employed appealed to the nature of God. What purpose could God possibly have in creating innumerable worlds, they asked, unless it were to populate them with sentient beings such as ourselves? Otherwise, they implied, the infinite power and love of God would be going to waste, which would be an utterly incomprehensible state of affairs.

Logicians and philosophers point out many perplexing difficulties with analogical reasoning. So it is to Swedenborg's credit that he did not base his statements about extraterrestrials on arguments from analogy. Nor did he base them on a transcendent intuition concerning how God ought to behave. Of course, he acknowledged that the existence of intelligent life throughout the universe flowed from the infinite beneficence of God, but there is a major difference of emphasis. He begins *Life on Other Planets* by saying "Since . . . I was desirous of knowing whether there were other inhabited worlds, and what they and their inhabitants were like, I was allowed by the Lord to talk and mix with spirits and angels from other worlds" (§1). In other words, he knows that there are extraterrestrials because of a personal experience of interacting and communicating with them. And he could interact and communicate with them because he shared a spiritual bond with them, through God. It is this that distinguishes Swedenborg from the other great thinkers of his era who also asserted that intelligent creatures inhabit other worlds in outer space.

Thomas Wright (1711–1786), Johann Lambert (1728–1777), Immanuel Kant (1724–1804), and William Herschel (1738–1822) were pre-eminent authorities on astronomy in the eighteenth century. All these men affirmed that there were innumerable inhabited worlds in space, although they held this belief for different and even divergent reasons. Historically, Kant overshadows the others, whose accomplishments have faded into relative obscurity. Kant's thoughts on extraterrestrial intelligence naturally invite comparison with what Swedenborg has to say in *Life on Other Planets.*

In *The Critique of Pure Reason* (1781), his magnum opus, Kant reaffirmed his "strong belief, on the correctness of which I would stake even many of the advantages of life, that there are inhabitants in other worlds."[4] It was an opinion he had maintained throughout his career. In *Universal Natural History and Theory of the Heavens* (1755),

---

4. Immanuel Kant, *Critique of Pure Reason,* trans. J.M.D. Meiklejohn (London: The Colonial Press, 1956), 468.

the foundational document of sidereal astronomy, Kant asserted that the other planets of our solar system are inhabited.

In that book, Kant theorized that planets form from rotating discs of gas and other material that surround newly formed stars. The planets closer to the star condense from a cruder grade of material, while those farther away from the sun are made of a more refined sort of matter that was, by implication, more perfect. In that scheme of things, the farther a planet is from its star, the higher the intellectual level of its inhabitants. As Kant put it, "The excellence of thinking natures . . . stands under a certain rule, according to which these become more excellent and perfect in proportion to the distance of their habitats from the sun."[5]

Accordingly, Kant's Mercurians and Venusians have only a rudimentary intellectual faculty, one that is inferior to that of earthlings. The inhabitants of Earth, he held, are on "exactly the middle rung" as far as rational intellect is concerned. He claimed that the inhabitants of the outer planets, such as Jupiter and Saturn, are far superior in intellect to the inhabitants of Earth. They may even be so advanced, he believed, that they are relatively immune to death.

Kant kept extraterrestrials in mind when he propounded one of the most renowned tenets of his philosophy. He intended the categorical imperative, the fundamental principle of his theory of morals, to apply to all rational beings throughout the universe. So, like

5. Immanuel Kant, *Universal Natural History and Theory of the Heavens,* trans. William Hastie (Ann Arbor, Mich.: University of Michigan Press, 1969), 189.

Swedenborg, he contended that we exist in a spiritual relationship with sentient creatures on other worlds.

Ideas similar to many of those found in *Life on Other Planets* were in the air during the eighteenth century. For instance, William Herschel, the celebrated founder of observational stellar astronomy, was convinced that the moon was inhabited, and Kant fully concurred. Clearly, Swedenborg's espousal of lunarians was not unusual for a learned man of his era.

Herschel even asserted that the sun and stars were inhabited and offered definite descriptions of the beings who lived there. Johann Lambert wrote a book claiming that comets were inhabited. So Swedenborg appears as a moderate on issues pertaining to extraterrestrial life when *Life on Other Planets* is placed in its historical context.

Scientific knowledge relating to other solar systems is expanding so rapidly that it is difficult to extrapolate what will happen next. Even so, astronomers may detect extraterrestrial civilizations much sooner than most of us anticipate. Swedenborg's thoughts about sentient extraterrestrials may well appear in a startling new light in the not-too-distant future. It is reasonable to expect that the importance and influence of *Life on Other Planets* will continue to grow. It is quite probable, in my judgment, that unfolding events will someday add another distinction to Swedenborg's record of historic accomplishments. In the future, he may well be looked upon as the intellectual forefather of a science of communicating with intelligent extraterrestrial beings.

Dr. Raymond Moody
Anniston, Alabama

A Note on This Text

Life on Other Planets, one of Emanuel Swedenborg's most controversial works, has rarely been published outside of Swedenborg's collected writings. In 1997, however, the Swedenborg Society in London published a new translation by the eminent linguist and classical scholar John Chadwick, under the title *The Worlds in Space*. The present volume employs this translation.

Because of this, the American reader will find some unusual spellings and grammatical usages, since no changes to the text, whether in spelling, wording, or punctuation, have been made—with one exception, the use of double quotation marks for direct quotations.

Swedenborg was methodical in recording his experiences, even going so far as to reference other of his published works to explain and document some of his more arcane findings. At the back of the present volume, the reader will find "Author's Notes," which are indeed the original notes that Swedenborg supplied in the first edition of his text; these refer back to passages in *Secrets of Heaven* where he explained his tenets at greater length. Occasionally, he would repeat a note, which may cause some confusion for the current reader. The endnotes do not follow a sequential order throughout the text—for example, chapter 1 has endnotes 1 through 8, but the first endnote of chapter 2 is number 6. This is not an error; it indicates that endnote 6 was repeated in Swedenborg's original text.

All notes appearing at the bottom of a page are those of John Chadwick and are followed by the initials TR.

John Chadwick (1920–1998) is little known outside of classical academia. However, within that rarified sphere, Chadwick was lauded as the decipherer, along with Michael Ventris, of Linear B, the script of the Mycenaean civilization, an early form of Greek. For over thirty years, he was a lecturer in classics at Cambridge University, during which time he also managed to write the landmark books *The Decipherment of Linear B* and *The Mycenaean World.*

John Chadwick was an avid and appreciative reader of the works of Emanuel Swedenborg. In addition to the translation of the present work, he also translated Swedenborg's *The True Christian Religion, The New Jerusalem and Its Heavenly Doctrine,* and *Conjugial Love,* among others, for the Swedenborg Society and compiled and edited the exhaustive *A Lexicon to the Latin Texts of the Theological Writings of Emanuel Swedenborg (1688–1772),* affectionately referred to as "Chadwick's Lexicon," a concordance/dictionary of words found in Swedenborg's writings.

Life on
Other Planets

The Worlds In Space

1. By the Lord's Divine mercy I have had my interior faculties, which belong to my spirit, opened, so that I have been enabled to talk with spirits and angels, not only those in the vicinity of our earth, but also with those near other worlds. Since therefore I was desirous of knowing whether there were other inhabited worlds, and what they and their inhabitants were like, I was allowed by the Lord to talk and mix with spirits and angels from other worlds. With some this lasted a day, with others a week, with yet others for months. I was informed by them about the worlds they came from and in the vicinity of which they were, about the life, behaviour and religious practices of their inhabitants, and other matters worth relating about them. Since I was allowed to gain my knowledge in this fashion, I can describe them from what I have heard and seen.

(2) It needs to be known that all spirits and angels are from the human race[1]; they are near their own world,[2] and know what happens there; and they can inform someone whose interior faculties are open sufficiently to be able to talk and mix with them. A human being is in essence a spirit,[3] and associates with spirits at the interior level.[4] Consequently anyone whose interior faculties are opened by the Lord can talk with them, exactly as a man can with another man.[5] I have been permitted to do this daily for the last twelve years.

2. It is a very well-known fact in the next life that there are many worlds inhabited by human beings, and there are spirits and angels who have come from them. Anyone there, whose desire springs from a love of truth and the purpose it can serve, is permitted to talk with spirits from other worlds, so as to get proof of the multiplicity of worlds. He can thus learn that the human race does not come from only one world, but from countless worlds; and moreover what these peoples' character is and how they live, and what sort of religious worship they practise.

3. I have held several discussions on this subject with spirits from our world, and I have been told that anyone of sound intellect can deduce from many facts known to him that there are many worlds and people living on them. For it is reasonable to infer that such vast bodies as the planets, some of which are larger than the earth, are not empty masses, created merely to circle the sun and shine their feeble light for the benefit of one world, but they must have some more important purpose than this. Anyone who believes, as each one of us should, that the Deity's sole purpose in creating the universe was to bring into existence the human race, and from this to people heaven—the human race being the seed-bed of heaven—must inevitably believe that, where there is a world, there must be human beings.

(2) The planets visible to our eyes, because they lie within the bounds of the solar system, can be plainly known to be worlds, as being bodies made of earthly matter. This is plain because they reflect sunlight and when seen through telescopes do not show the redness of flame as stars do, but are mottled with dark patches like lands on earth. Another argument is that they revolve around the sun in the same way as the earth, advancing along the path of the zodiac, and so causing years and seasons of the year, spring, summer, autumn and winter. They also rotate about their axes in the same way as the earth, thus causing days and the different periods of the day, morning, midday, evening and night. Moreover, some of them have moons, which are called satellites, travelling around their orbits with fixed periodicity, like the moon around the earth. The planet Saturn, being the furthest from the sun, has also a great shining ring which supplies that world with a great deal of light, even if it is reflected light. Can anyone knowing this and able to think rationally still claim that these are empty masses?

4. I have moreover discussed with spirits the argument that one can be led to infer that the universe contains more than one world from the fact that the starry sky is so immense and contains countless stars, each of which is a sun for its own region or system, resembling our sun, though differing in size. Anyone who correctly weighs these facts must conclude that the whole of this immense structure is a means to serve the ultimate purpose of creation, the establishment of a heavenly kingdom in which the Deity can dwell with angels and human beings. For the visible universe, that is, the sky shining with countless stars, each being a sun, is but a means to the creation of worlds, and human beings to live on them, from whom the heavenly kingdom may be formed. These facts must inevitably lead a reasonable person to think that so immense a means designed for so great a purpose could not have been made for the benefit of the human race, and the heaven from it, coming from one world. How would this appear to the Deity, who is infinite, to whom thousands, or rather tens of thousands, of worlds, all full of inhabitants, would seem trifling and almost negligible?

5. Moreover, the heaven of angels is so immense that it answers to every single part of the human body, tens of thousands of individuals to every single member, organ and internal part, and to every one of its affections. I have been allowed to know that there is no way that such a heaven with all its correspondences could have come into existence without drawing on the inhabitants of very many worlds.[6]

6. There are spirits whose sole interest is in acquiring knowledge, for this is the only thing that gives them pleasure. These spirits are therefore allowed to travel around, and also to go outside the solar system and visit others to acquire knowledge. They told me that there are worlds inhabited by human beings not only in this solar system, but beyond it in the starry sky, and in countless numbers. These spirits come from the planet Mercury.

7. As regards the religious worship of the inhabitants of other worlds, it is generally true that those of them who are not idolaters all acknowledge the Lord as the sole God.

They worship the Deity not as something invisible, but in visible form, because in fact when the Deity appears to them, He does so in human form, as He did once to Abraham and others in this world.[7] All who worship the Deity in human form are acceptable to the Lord.[8] They say too that no one can properly worship God, much less be linked to Him, without having some idea of Him which can be grasped; and this is only possible if He has human form. Without this the inner sight, which is the power of thinking about God, would be lost, just as is the sight of the eye when fixed upon the boundless expanse of space. Thought then could not help slipping into the idea of God as Nature, and then this would be worshipped as a god.

8. When they were told that on our earth the Lord took on Himself human nature, they pondered for a while; and then said that this was done to save the human race.

The World or Planet Mercury, and Its Spirits and Inhabitants

9. The whole heaven is in the form of a single human being, who is therefore called the Grand Man. Every detail, both outward and inward, in the human being answers to that Grand Man, that is, to heaven. This is a secret so far unknown in the world, but I have shown the truth of it at great length.[6] But those who reach heaven from our world are not enough to make up that Grand Man, being relatively few, so there will need to be people from many other worlds. The Lord's providence ensures that as soon as a deficiency in quality or quantity occurs at any point in the correspondence, people are instantly summoned from another world to fill up the numbers, so maintaining the proportion and keeping heaven stable.

10. I have also had disclosed to me from heaven the part played by the spirits from the planet Mercury in forming the Grand Man. It is the memory, but it is the memory of ideas abstracted from earthly and purely material objects. However, having been allowed to talk with them over a period of many weeks, hearing what they are like and how things are with the inhabitants of that world, I should like to relate my actual experiences.

11. Some spirits approached me, and I was told from heaven that they were from the world nearest to the sun, the planet named in our world Mercury. Immediately on arrival they sought out from my memory what I knew. (Spirits are very clever at doing this, being able when they approach a person to see the details stored in his memory.[9]) So when they looked into various matters, including the cities and places I had visited, I noticed that they were not interested in churches, palaces, houses or streets, but only in the events I knew had taken place in them, together with such matters as their administration, the character and customs of their inhabitants, and so forth. For such matters are closely bound up with places in a person's memory, so that when the places are recalled, these facts are presented too. I was surprised at this behaviour, so I asked why they dismissed the splendid locations and only looked into the things and events associated with them. They said that they took no pleasure in looking at material, bodily or earthly objects, but only facts. This proved that the spirits from that world answer to the memory of abstract ideas, not material or earthly ones.

12. I was told that the inhabitants of that world behaved in the same way. That is to say, they take no interest in earthly or bodily matters, but in the constitutions, laws and

governments of peoples. They are also interested in heavenly matters, which are innumerable. I was also told that
many of the people of that world converse with spirits, so
that they know about spiritual matters and the conditions
of life after death, which makes them disdain bodily and
earthly matters. For anyone who knows for sure and is
convinced he will live after death is concerned about heavenly matters, since they are an everlasting source of happiness, but not about worldly matters, except so far as the
necessities of life demand it. This being the nature of the
inhabitants, it is also that of the spirits who come from
there.[2]

13. The following experience proved to me how anxious
they are to seek out and absorb knowledge of the kind to
be found in the levels of the memory above bodily sense-
perceptions. When they were looking into my knowledge
of heavenly matters, they ran through everything and kept
saying: "That's the sort of thing, that's it." For when spirits approach a person, they review everything in his memory, calling up from it whatever suits them. In fact, as I
have often observed, they read its contents as if it were a
book.[10] These spirits used to do this more skilfully and
faster, because they skipped the things that slow down and
narrow the inward sight, so as to delay it. All earthly and
bodily matters are in this class, if they are regarded as ends
in themselves, if, that is, they alone are loved. They concentrate on real objects. For objects free from earthly en-
cumbrance allow the mind to rise and expand widely; but
purely material objects draw it downwards, restricting and
closing it.

Another experience which plainly showed their anxiety
to acquire knowledge and enrich their memory was this. I

was once writing something about future events, and they were then too far off to look into these by drawing them out of my memory. They were very cross because I was unwilling to read those things in their presence, and contrary to their usual habit they wanted to abuse me, calling me very wicked, and similar names. So as to show their annoyance they brought on a kind of painful contraction of the right side of my head as far as the ear. But such efforts did me no harm. Since, however, they had done wrong, they kept withdrawing even farther, but still kept stopping, because they wanted to know what I had written. That is how anxious they are for knowledge.

14. The spirits of Mercury surpass others in the amount of knowledge they possess, both about matters within the solar system and in the starry sky beyond it. What they have once learned they retain, and recall whenever similar facts are observed. This is another clear proof that spirits have a memory, one in fact much more perfect than human beings have. They retain what they see, hear or otherwise grasp, especially if they get pleasure from it, as these spirits do from knowledge. Things that give pleasure and are loved flow in as if of their own accord and are retained. Other things do not penetrate the memory, but only make superficial contact and slip away.

15. When the spirits of Mercury visit other communities, they investigate the extent of their knowledge, and having done so depart. There exists among spirits, especially among angels, a means of communication which ensures that, if they are in a community where they are accepted and loved, everything they know is shared.[11]

16. The spirits of Mercury are more than usually proud of their knowledge. So they were told that, even though they knew countless facts, there is still an infinite number they do not know; and even if they went on increasing their knowledge for ever, they could still not achieve an acquaintance with all general principles. As for being proud and puffed up, they were told this was not proper. But they replied, by way of excusing their faults, that it was not pride, but merely boasting about the excellence of their memory.

17. They dislike speaking aloud because it is a physical process. So, when there were no spirits to act as intermediaries, I was only able to talk with them by a kind of thought activation. Their memory, being of ideas, not of purely material pictures, presents these more directly to their thinking. For thinking above the pictorial level needs abstract ideas as its object. For all this the spirits of Mercury are not particularly distinguished for their powers of judgment. They take no pleasure in matters requiring judgment or in inferences from known facts. It is the bare facts that give them pleasure.

18. They were asked whether they did not want to make some use of their knowledge, since it is not enough to take pleasure in knowledge, but this must serve a purpose, which is its end in view. Knowledge alone would not serve any purpose for them, but would for others, if they were willing to share their knowledge with them. They were told that anyone who wants to be considered wise ought never to stop at acquiring knowledge, since these are merely auxiliary causes intended to assist the discovery of matters that will affect behaviour. But they replied that they take pleasure in acquiring knowledge, and that is for them its purpose.

19. Some of them do not want to be seen as human beings like the spirits from other worlds, but as crystal globes. The reason why they want to be seen thus, although they do not succeed, is that in the next life knowledge of non-material matters is represented by crystals.

20. The spirits of Mercury are totally different from the spirits of our world, since these are not so much interested in ideas as in worldly, bodily and earthly matters, which are material objects. For this reason the spirits of Mercury are unable to associate with the spirits of our world, and wherever they meet them, they run away. The spiritual spheres which emanate from either party are more or less antagonistic. The spirits of Mercury claim that they do not wish to look at the wrapping, but the ideas stripped of their wrappings, that is, what is inside.

21. A fairly bright flame was to be seen burning cheerfully; it lasted for some time. The flame signalled the arrival of spirits from Mercury whose perception, thought and speech were quicker than that of the previous ones. Immediately on arrival they ran through the contents of my memory, but they were too quick for me to grasp what it was they were observing. I heard them saying repeatedly: "That's the sort of thing." When they came to what I had seen in the heavens and in the world of spirits, they said they had known this before. I became aware of a large number of spirits associated with them, who were behind me, a little to the left on a level with the back of the head.

22. On another occasion I saw a large number of spirits of this kind, but at some distance from myself, in front and a little to the right. From there they talked with me, but using spirits as intermediaries, for their speech is as rapid as thought and can only be translated into human language by using other spirits as intermediaries. What surprised me was that their speech gave an impression of a rolling wave,* but was still so ready and quick. Since there were many of them speaking at once their speech reached me in waves. A remarkable feature was that it slipped towards my left eye, though they were standing to my right. This was because the left eye corresponds to knowledge of abstract ideas, matters, that is, which are in the province of intelligence; the right eye corresponds to matters which are in the province of wisdom.[12] They displayed the same quickness in grasping what they had heard and in taking decisions as they did in speaking. They kept saying: "Yes, that's right; no, that isn't," making virtually instantaneous judgments.

23. There was a spirit from another world who could talk with them with dexterity, because he spoke so readily and quickly, but he made a point of elegance in his discourse. They arrived at instant judgments about what he said, saying one expression was too elegant, another too clever. But in doing so, they only paid attention to whether they heard anything from him they did not already know. In that way they rejected anything that caused obscurity, especially efforts at elegant discourse and displays of learning, since these conceal the real ideas, substituting for them words which are the expressions of material objects. For the speaker concentrates on these and wants his words to be

---

* The precise meaning of this word is not clear, but a parallel passage in *Spiritual Diary* §3233 adds: "there was as it were a roll of them talking at once".—TR.

listened to rather than what the words mean, so that he has more effect on the other's hearing than on his mind.

24. The spirits from the world of Mercury do not keep to any one place, or within the groups of spirits belonging to one world, but travel through the universe. This is because they answer to the memory of facts, which they are continually trying to enrich. So they are permitted to travel around and acquire for themselves knowledge wherever they can. On their travels, if they meet spirits who love material, that is, bodily and earthly matters, they avoid them and go off somewhere where they do not hear such subjects mentioned. This is a proof that their minds are raised above the level of sense-impressions, so that they enjoy inward illumination. I was also allowed to perceive this for myself, when they were near and talking with me. I noticed then that I was being withdrawn from sense-impressions, so much so that my physical sight started to become dim and blurred.

25. The spirits of that world go about in platoons and squadrons, and when they are assembled they form a kind of globe. They are so linked by the Lord that they act as one, and the knowledge of each is shared with all, and that of all with each individual, as happens in heaven.[11] Another proof that they travel through the universe to acquire factual knowledge was afforded me by the fact that once, when they seemed to me a long way off, they spoke to me from there and said that they were then assembled and were travelling outside the system of this world into the starry heaven; they knew that there were to be found there people who care nothing for earthly or bodily matters, but ones above these, and it was these people with whom they wished to be. It was said that they do not know themselves where they are going, but by Divine guidance they are directed to places where they can learn about what they do not yet know, but which fits in with the knowledge they already have. It was also said that they do not know either how to find the companions who join them, but this too happens by Divine guidance.

26. Since they are travellers through the universe and so especially able to know about systems and worlds outside the solar system, I discussed this subject with them. They said that the universe contains very many worlds inhabited by human beings. They were surprised that anyone was what they called so lacking in judgment as to think that almighty God's heaven was composed of spirits and angels coming from one world, when compared with the omnipotence of God these were so few as to be hardly anything, even if there were many thousands of systems and many thousands of worlds. They went on to say that they knew of the existence of more than several hundred thousand worlds in the universe; and yet this is nothing to the infinite Deity.

27. When the spirits of Mercury were with me while I was writing an explanation of the Word in its internal sense, and they could tell what I was writing, they said that what I was writing was extremely gross, almost all the expressions seeming to be material. But I was allowed to reply that people in our world still look upon my writings as so subtle and high-flown, that they are unable to grasp much of them. I went on to say that many people in this world are unaware that there is an inner man which acts upon the outer man and causes him to be alive; but they convince themselves from delusive sense-impressions that the body possesses life. As a result those who are wicked and lacking in faith cast doubt on life after death. They also call the part of a person which survives death not a spirit, but a soul. They dispute what the soul is and where it is located, believing that it must be rejoined to the material body, even though this has been scattered to the four winds, for a person to continue living as a person; and much more of the same sort.

On hearing this the spirits of Mercury asked whether such people could become angels. I was allowed to answer that those who had lived good lives of faith and charity did become angels, being no longer concerned with outward and material affairs, but with inward and spiritual ones. When they reach that state, they enjoy light surpassing that of the spirits from Mercury. To enable them to know that this is so, an angel from the heaven formed from our world, who had lived this sort of life in the world, was allowed to talk with them. More will be said about this later.

28. Afterwards the spirits of Mercury sent me a long piece of paper of irregular shape, being a number of sheets glued together, which looked to be printed in the sort of type used in this world. I asked whether they had papers like this in their world; they said no, but they knew such papers existed in our world. They were unwilling to say more; but I perceived that they thought knowledge in our world was committed to paper rather than to people, poking fun at us as if papers knew things that people do not. But they were informed what is the truth about this. Some time later they came back and sent me another paper, also printed like the previous one, not glued together and untidy, but clean and neat. They said that they had received further information that in this world papers existed such as this, from which books are made.

29. What I have said so far proves clearly that spirits retain in their memory what they see and hear in the next life, and that they can be taught just as much as when they were human beings in the world; and this applies equally to matters of faith, so that they can become more perfect. The more inward spirits and angels are, the more readily and fully they absorb what they learn and the more exactly they retain it. Since this process continues for ever, it is evident that their wisdom continually increases. In the case of the spirits from Mercury their knowledge of facts continually increases, but this does not cause an increase of wisdom, because they love knowledge, which is a means, rather than the purposes to which it should be put, which are the ends it serves.

30. Further evidence for the character of the spirits from the planet Mercury will be presented in the following sections. It needs to be known that, however many spirits and angels there are, they were all once human beings. The human race is the seed-bed of heaven. Spirits have exactly the same affections and inclinations as they had when they lived as human beings in this world. For everyone's life accompanies him.[13] This being so, it is possible to know the character of the people of any world by reference to the spirits from it.

31. Since the spirits of Mercury answer to the memory of abstract, non-material ideas in the Grand Man, they are unwilling to listen when anyone talks with them about earthly, bodily and purely worldly matters. If they are obliged to listen to these subjects, they change them into something else, very often their opposites, in order to escape them.

32. To prove to me that this was their character, I was allowed to show them pictures of meadows, ploughed fields, gardens, woods and rivers. (Showing pictures of such things is done by presenting them to others by use of the imagination; in the next life these look exactly like the real things.) But they immediately changed these, making the meadows and fields dark and filling them with snakes by picturing them. They turned the rivers black, so that the water was not transparent. When I asked them why they did this, they replied that they were unwilling to think about such things, but only real things, that is, the knowledge of abstract subjects, particularly those which arise in the heavens.

33. Later I showed them pictures of the kinds of birds, both large and small, to be found in our world. Lifelike pictures of such things can be shown in the next life. On seeing these birds pictured, at first they wanted to change them, but then they were pleased with them and became quiet. This was because birds mean the knowledge of facts, a thing they perceived by means of an influence they then felt.[14] So they stopped changing them so as to avoid taking them into their memory. Later I was allowed to picture to them a most beautiful garden full of lamps and lanterns. Then they paused and their attention was caught, because lamps together with lanterns mean truths shining as the result of good.[15] This made it plain that they could be kept watching material objects, so long as at the same time their meaning in the spiritual sense was hinted at. What is conveyed by the spiritual sense is not completely abstract, since it is represented by these objects.

34. I also talked with them about sheep and lambs, but they would not listen, because they perceived such things as earthly. This was because they did not understand what innocence is, which is what lambs mean. I grasped this from their saying, when I told them that lambs in heaven mean innocence,[16] that they knew innocence as a word, but not what it meant. This is because they are only fond of knowledge, not of the purposes which items of knowledge must serve; so neither were they able to know what innocence is by inward perception.

35. Some spirits from Mercury visited me who had been sent by other spirits to hear what was going on around me. One of the spirits from our world told them to tell their own people not to speak anything but the truth, and not to follow their custom of replying to questions by stating the opposite. If any of the spirits from our world, he said, were to do this, he would be beaten. The answer came back from the distant group which had sent the spirits that, if that deserved a beating, then they should all be beaten, since they were so much in the habit of doing this they could not stop. They said that this is also what they do when talking to people in their world, but they do not intend to deceive them, but rather to instill a desire for knowledge. For when they state the opposite and go some way towards hiding the matter, then the desire to know is aroused and the memory is sharpened by their anxiety to find it out.

I also had a conversation with them on the same subject on another occasion. Knowing that they talked with people in their world, I asked how they teach its inhabitants. They said that they do not teach them what is the fact of the matter, but they give them a hint of it, so as to nurture and increase their desire to find out and know the fact. For if they replied to every question, the desire would disappear.

They went on to say that another reason why they state the opposite is to show up the truth better; for every truth shows up best when contrasted with its opposite.

36. It is their custom not to tell anyone what they know, yet they want to learn from everyone what he knows. But they share all their knowledge with their own community, to the point that all know what one knows, and each one there knows what all know.

37. The spirits of Mercury are rather proud of how much they know. This makes them think that, since they know so much, there can hardly be any more to know. But they were told by spirits from our world that their knowledge is not extensive but limited, and what they do not know is comparatively speaking infinite. They said that, compared with what they knew, what they did not know was like the waters of a mighty ocean compared with those of a tiny spring. The first step towards wisdom, they said, was to know, acknowledge and perceive that what a person knows is so small compared with what he does not know as to be scarcely anything.

To prove to them that this was so, an angelic spirit was permitted to talk with them, telling them in general terms what they knew and did not know, and asserting that there were infinite things they did not know, and all eternity would not be enough to learn even the general principles. He spoke in angelic ideas, much more readily than they did, and they were amazed to find that he could disclose what they knew and what they did not know.

Later I saw another angel speaking with them; he was to be seen at some height towards the right. He came from our world. He went through a long list of things they did not know; and then talked with them by means of changes of state, something they said they did not understand. So he told them that each change of state contained an infinite number of things, as also did the smallest detail of a change. On hearing this they began to humble themselves, having previously been so proud of their knowledge. Their self-abasement was pictured by the letting down of their roll (for their group then appeared in the form of a roll, in front towards the left at a distance, on a level with the region below the navel.) The roll looked as if sagging in the middle but high at both sides. I could observe some to-and-fro movement taking place in it, and they were told the meaning of this; it showed what they were thinking in their state of self-abasement, while those high up at the sides were not yet humbling themselves. I saw the roll divide, those not humbling themselves being banished back towards their own globe, while the remainder stayed.

38. Spirits from Mercury came to visit a certain spirit from our world, who had been famous for his learning while living in the world, wanting to learn about various matters from him. (He was Christian Wolf.*) But they saw that what he said was not raised above the sense-impressions of the natural man, because in speaking he thought about his reputation, and he wanted, as he had in the world (everyone retaining the same character in the next life), to string together various matters, and to link them again with others, leading continually to new conclusions. Since he tried to produce long chains of arguments based on matters which they did not see or acknowledge as true, they said that the chains did not hang together nor did they lead to his conclusions, calling them the obscurity of authority. So

---

*Johann Christian von Wolf, 1679–1754, a German philosopher who was influential in the eighteenth century.—TR.

then they stopped questioning him, only asking: "What is this called? What is that?" Since his replies to these questions were couched in material ideas with no spirituality in them, they left him. Everyone in the next life speaks the more spiritually, or in spiritual ideas, the more he has in the world believed in God, and in material ideas the more he has failed to believe in Him.

(2) I should like to take the opportunity this offers to bring in here an experience which shows what happens in the next life to learned men who acquire intelligence from their own reflection fired by a love of knowing truths for their own sake, and so for purposes remote from mundane considerations; and also what happens to those who seek to acquire intelligence from other people without reflecting for themselves, as do those whose wish to learn truths is only to gain a reputation for learning, and so to acquire honours or advantages in the world, not, that is, for unworldly purposes.

I became aware of a sound penetrating from below near my left side and reaching up to my left ear. I realised that there were spirits there trying to struggle free, though what sort of spirits they were I could not tell. But when they had struggled out, they talked with me, and said they were logicians and metaphysicians. They had, they said, plunged into deep thought on these subjects, but with no other motive than that of being called learned, and so achieving honours and wealth. They complained that they now led a miserable life, because they had no other purpose in studying these subjects, so that they had not by their means cultivated their rational faculty. Their speech was slow and had a muffled sound.

(3) Meanwhile two spirits carried on a conversation over my head, and when I asked who they were, I was told

that one of them was a very famous character in the world of letters, and I was given to believe that it was Aristotle. (I was not told who the other was.) He was then put into the state he had been in while living in the world. Anyone can easily be returned to the state he had in the world, because he carries with him every state in his life. To my surprise he approached my right ear and spoke there, hoarsely, but sensibly. I was able to tell from the feel of his speech that he was of quite a different character from the scholastics who had come up first; in fact he had drawn on his own thinking in what he wrote and in devising his philosophy. Thus the terms which he invented and imposed on ideas thought about were forms of words to describe inward ideas. He had also, as I learned, been impelled to these discoveries by the pleasure he took in them and the longing to know matters relating to thinking and the intellect; and he had obediently followed the dictates of his spirit. This was why he approached my right ear, unlike his followers, known as scholastics, who do not proceed from thought to terms, but from terms to thought, which is the wrong way. Many of them do not even proceed as far as thought, restricting themselves to the terms. If they make use of these, it is to prove whatever they wish, and to impart to falsities the appearance of truth, to suit what they wish people to believe. Philosophy thus becomes for them the route to madness rather than to wisdom, and plunges them into darkness instead of light.

(4) I then discussed with him the science of analysis. I said that a small boy could say more philosophically, analytically and logically in half an hour than Aristotle had been able to say in a book*, because the whole of human

---

*Probably a reference to Aristotle's two works known as *Analytics*.— Tr.

thought and the speech it produces is analytical, being governed by laws derived from the spiritual world. Anyone who wanted to proceed artificially from terms to thought was rather like a dancer, who tries to use his knowledge of motor fibres and muscles in order to dance; if he concentrated on that while he was dancing, he would hardly be able to move his foot. In fact, without any such knowledge he can move all the motor fibres scattered throughout the body, and appropriately activate his lungs, diaphragm, flanks, arms, neck and so on, which whole books would not be enough to describe. I said that the case of those who sought to make terms the basis of their thinking was much the same. He approved of this, and remarked that learning to think by this route was proceeding the wrong way round. If anyone wanted to be a fool, that was the way to go about it; but he ought to think constantly about the purpose and take an inward view.

(5) He then showed me what had been his conception of the supreme power, which he had pictured to himself as having a human face with the head surrounded by a radiant halo. He now knew, he said, that that person is the Lord and the radiant halo is the Divine proceeding from Him, which flows not only into heaven but into the universe, controlling and ordering both. He who controls and orders heaven does the same to the universe, since the one cannot be separated from the other. He also said that he had believed in only one God, but that he distinguished His attributes and qualities by as many names as others worshipped gods.

(6) A woman appeared to me, who put out her hand wishing to stroke my cheek. When I expressed surprise, he said that when he was in the world he had often had such a woman appear to him and seem to stroke his cheek; and

she had a beautiful hand. The angelic spirits said that once upon a time the early people had seen such women and gave them the name of Pallas. She appeared, they said, to one of the spirits who in antiquity had taken great pleasure in ideas, and devoted themselves to thinking, but not to philosophy. Since such spirits had been present with him and had been pleased with him for basing his thinking on an inward view, they had caused such a woman to be presented to view.

(7) Lastly he sketched his idea about the human soul or spirit, which he called *pneuma*.* He thought of this as a vital principle, invisible as a piece of the ether. He said that he had known that his spirit would live on after death, since it was his inward essence, which cannot die because it can think. Beyond that he had been unable to think clearly, having only dim ideas because he had no knowledge about it other than what he thought out for himself, and even the ancients told him little. Aristotle, moreover, is among the sound spirits in the next life, while many of his followers are among the foolish.

39. I once saw some spirits from our world in company with spirits from Mercury, and heard them conversing. The spirits of our world asked them among other things, in whom they believed. They replied that they believed in God, but when asked further about the God they believed in, they were unwilling to answer, since it was not their habit to answer questions directly. Then the spirits from Mercury in their turn asked the spirits from our world in whom they believed. They said, in the Lord God. The spirits of Mercury then said that they could perceive that the others did not

---

*The Greek word for "breath", translated into Latin as *spiritus*, or "spirit."

believe in any God, but were in the habit of saying they believed, while still not believing. (The spirits of Mercury have highly developed powers of perception, due to their continually using these powers to seek out what others know.) The spirits from our world belonged to those who in the world made a profession of faith in accordance with the teaching of the church, but still did not live by their faith. In the next life those who do not live by their faith lose it, because it is not a part of the person.[17] On hearing this they fell silent, because the dawning of perception then granted to them made them acknowledge that this was so.

40. There were some spirits who had been told from heaven that the spirits of the world of Mercury had once been promised that they would see the Lord. So they were asked by the spirits around me whether they remembered that promise; they said that they did, but they did not know if the promise had been made in such terms that there was no doubt attached to it. While they were discussing this among themselves, the sun of heaven appeared to them. (The only ones who see the sun of heaven, which is the Lord, are those in the innermost or third heaven; the rest only see the light from it.) On seeing the sun they said that this was not the Lord God, because they had not seen His face. Meanwhile the spirits went on talking among themselves, but I did not hear what they said. Then the sun suddenly appeared again, with the Lord in its midst surrounded by a solar halo. On seeing this the spirits of Mercury made a profound obeisance and sank down. Then the Lord also appeared out of that sun to the spirits of this world also who, when people on earth, had seen Him in the world. Each of these, one after the other in a long series, asserted that it was the Lord Himself; this they did in the presence of all assembled. Then the Lord also appeared out of the sun to the spirits of the planet Jupiter; they asserted in plain terms, that it was He whom they had seen in their own world, when the God of the universe appeared to them.[18]

41. Some, after seeing the Lord, were conducted forward towards the right; and as they advanced they said they could see a much brighter and purer light than ever before, and no greater light could ever be seen. At the time it was evening here. There were many spirits who said this.[19]

42. It needs to be known that no spirit is able to see the sun of the world at all, or any light from it. The light of that sun is to spirits and angels like thick darkness. Spirits merely retain an idea of that sun from seeing it when in the world, and it is envisaged as a dark patch, behind and a long way off, in height slightly above head-level. The planets belonging to the solar system are to be seen in fixed positions relative to the sun. Mercury is behind, a little to the right; Venus to the left, a little behind; Mars in front to the left; Jupiter likewise to the left and in front, but further away; Saturn right in front at a very great distance. The moon is on the left, fairly high up; and the satellites of each planet are to the left of it. That is how spirits envisage their planets; and the spirits are to be seen in the vicinity of their own planet, but outside it. However, the spirits of Mercury in particular are not to be seen in a fixed direction or at a fixed distance; they appear now in front, now to the left, now a little behind. The reason is that they are allowed to travel around the universe to acquire knowledge.

43. The spirits of Mercury were once seen to the left in a globe, and then later this stretched out lengthwise to form a roll. I wondered where they wanted to go, whether it was to this world or somewhere else. Shortly afterwards I observed that they were turning to the right and rotating until they approached the world or planet Venus, at its forward face*. But on reaching there they said they did not want to be there, because the people were wicked. So they went around to the rear part of that world; then they said they wanted to stay there, because the people were good. While this was happening I felt a considerable change in my brain, and a strong activity coming from it. From this I was able to infer that the spirits of Venus who come from that region of the planet agreed with the spirits of Mercury, since they answer to the memory of material ideas, which agrees with the memory of non-material ideas to which the spirits of Mercury answer. Consequently, when they were there, the activity emanating from them was stronger.

44. Since I wished to know what the people of Mercury were like in face and body, whether they resemble people on our earth, a woman was displayed to my gaze, who was very much like women on earth. She had a comely face, but one smaller than women on our earth have. Her body too was more slender, though of similar height. She wore a linen scarf on her head, neatly but not elaborately arranged. A man was also displayed; he too had a more slender body than men of our world. He was wearing a dark blue garment, which fitted the body tightly, with no fold or protuberances on either side. I was told that this was the form and bodily habit of people belonging to that

---

* The parallel passage at *Arcana Coelestia* §7170 defines "forward" as the side turned away from the sun, and the "rear part" as that facing the sun.—TR.

world. I also saw their species of oxen and cows; they were not very different from those in our world, only smaller. They looked in a way rather like hinds and stags.

45. They were also asked what the sun of our world looks like from their world. They assured me that it was large and looked bigger there than from other worlds. They said they knew this by reference to the idea other spirits had of the sun. They went on to say that their climate was temperate, neither too hot nor too cold. I was allowed to tell them that this was the Lord's providence, to prevent an excess of heat due to their world being nearer the sun than the other planets. Heat is not the result of proximity to the sun, but depends on the thickness and density of the atmosphere, as is plain from high mountains being cold even in hot climates. Temperature is also regulated by the directness or obliquity of the incidence of the sun's rays, as is evident from the seasons of winter and summer in any one region.

This is what I have been allowed to learn about the spirits and inhabitants of the world of Mercury.

On the World or Planet Jupiter, and Its Spirits and Inhabitants

46. I was allowed to associate for a longer period with the spirits and angels of the planet Jupiter than with those from the other planets. I have therefore more to report about the way they and the inhabitants of that planet live. I had many indications, and it was told me from heaven, that these spirits were from that place.

47. The world or planet of Jupiter is not visible to spirits and angels. No one there can ever see a planet, only the spirits and angels who came from it. Those from Jupiter are to be seen in front to the left at a considerable distance, and they constantly keep this position (see §42 above). Their planet too is there. The spirits of each world are in the vicinity of their own planet, because they come from its inhabitants. (Every person after death becomes a spirit.) Being of similar character, they are able to associate with the inhabitants and be of service to them.

48. They related that in the region of the planet where they lived while in the world there was a large population, as large as the planet could feed. The land was fertile and abounded in all kinds of produce. But people there did not wish for more than was necessary to live. They could not see the use of what was not necessary, and this was why the population was so large. They said that their chief concern was the bringing up of children, whom they loved most tenderly.

49. They went on to tell me that they are divided into tribes, families and households, each of which live in separate groups composed only of their own people. As a result they associate only with their kinsfolk. No one ever covets another's property, so it never occurs to anyone to desire anything which is another's, much less to devise schemes for getting hold of it, still less to seize and plunder it. They regard this as a crime against human nature and therefore repulsive. When I wanted to tell them that in our world we have wars, plundering and murders, they turned their backs, and refused to listen.

(2) I was told by angels that the earliest people in this world lived in similar fashion, divided into tribes, families and households. They were then all content with their own property, and it was unheard of to get rich at the expense of others' property, or selfishly to dominate others. For this reason ancient times, and especially the most ancient period, were more pleasing to the Lord than those which followed. Since such was their state, there was a reign of innocence coupled with wisdom. Everyone then did good

out of goodness and honest deeds out of honesty. They did not know what it was to do good and honest deeds for one's own reputation or advantage. Then too they spoke nothing but the truth, not so much for truth's sake as because of goodness; that is to say, their motive came not from the intellectual faculty acting alone, but from the voluntary faculty combined with the intellectual. Such were ancient times, so that angels could then mix with human beings, and virtually lift their minds out of bodily thoughts and carry them off into heaven. In fact, they could take them touring around heaven, showing off its magnificence and happiness, sharing with them their own happiness and pleasures. The ancient writers too knew about this period and called it the Golden Age or the reign of Saturn.

(3) The reason the period was like this was, as I said, that they lived divided into tribes, the tribes divided into families, and these into households, each household living by itself. Then it never occurred to anyone to seize another's inheritance in order to acquire wealth from it or power. Selfishness and love of the world were unknown. Every one was happy with his own property, and no less happy at other people's property. But as time went on, this scene changed and turned into its opposite, when men's minds were seized with the greed for power and great possessions. Then to protect itself the human race grouped itself into kingdoms and empires. Since the laws of charity and conscience, which men had had inscribed on their hearts, ceased to operate, it became necessary to pass legislation to control violent acts, so as to reward observance with honours and advantages and disobedience with punishments. This brought about so great a change that heaven itself moved away from men, retreating further and further down to the present age, when people no longer

know whether heaven or hell exist, and some actually deny their existence. The purpose of these remarks is to illustrate by a parallel the condition of the people of the world of Jupiter, and to show where their uprightness and wisdom too come from. More will be said about this in what follows.

50. My long continued association with the spirits of Jupiter proved to me that they are more upright than the spirits of many other worlds. When they arrived, their coming, their stay and the influence they exerted were so gentle and sweet as to defy expression. In the next life the character of each spirit reveals itself in his influence, which is a sharing of his affection. Uprightness is revealed by gentleness and sweetness, by gentleness because he is fearful of doing harm, and by sweetness because he loves to do good. I could very clearly tell apart the gentleness and sweetness of good spirits from our world from that of theirs. They said that when any mild dispute arises between them, there is to be seen a kind of thin shaft of light, such as lightning often produces, or a band filled with flashing and moving stars. But a dispute among them is quickly settled. Stars which flash and at the same time move indicate falsity; flashing stars which are fixed indicate truth. So the former type indicates a dispute.[20]

51. I could recognise the presence of spirits from Jupiter not only by the gentleness and sweetness with which they arrived and made their influence felt, but also by the fact that their influence was exerted as much as possible on my face, making me look cheerful and smiling, for as long as they were present. They said that they do the same to the faces of the inhabitants of their world, when they visit them, wishing by this means to impart tranquillity and hearty joy. The tranquillity and joy they gave me I could feel filling my chest and heart. It took away the desires and anxieties about the future which cause disturbance and worry and fill the mind with varied emotions.

By this means I was able to establish what kind of life the inhabitants of Jupiter lead. The nature of the inhabitants can be known from that of the spirits, for each takes his own way of life with him from the world, and when he becomes a spirit lives in the same way. I noticed that they had a state of blessedness, an even more inward happiness. I noticed this by perceiving that their interiors were not closed to heaven, but open; and the more open to heaven one's interiors are, the easier it is for them to receive the goodness of God, which is accompanied by blessedness and inward happiness. It is quite different with those whose lives are not in accord with heaven's order, but have their interiors closed, and their exteriors open to the world.

52. I was also shown the kind of faces the inhabitants of the world of Jupiter have. I did not see the inhabitants themselves, but spirits looking as they had been when in their own world. But before this demonstration one of their angels appeared behind a shining cloud to grant permission. Two faces were then shown to me. They resembled the faces of people of our world, white and handsome, with a look of sincerity and modesty shining from them.

(2) While the spirits of Jupiter were with me, the faces of people of our world looked smaller than usual. This was due to the effect of the idea those spirits had that their own faces were larger. For while they live as human beings in their world, they have a belief that after death their faces

will be larger and round in shape. Since this idea has been impressed on them, it lasts, and when they become spirits they seem to themselves to have a larger face.

(3) The reason why they think their faces will be larger is that, according to them, the face is not part of the body, but is the part which enables them to see, hear and speak and express their thoughts. Thus the mind shines through the face, so that they think of the face as the shape taken by the mind. Knowing that they will be wiser after their life in the world, they think this means the shape of their mind and thus their face will be enlarged.

(4) They also believe that after death they will feel a fire which will warm their faces. Their reason for saying this is that the wiser among them know that fire in the spiritual sense means love; love is the fire of life, and it is this fire which gives life to angels.[21] Those of them who have lived in a state of heavenly love actually achieve their ambition; they feel their faces grow warm and the interiors of their minds are fired with love.

(5) For this reason the inhabitants of that world frequently wash and clean their faces, and take good care to protect them from sunburn. They have clothing made from bluish bark or cork, which they wrap around their heads to cover the face.

(6) On the subject of the faces of people of our world, which they saw through my eyes,[22] they said they were not handsome. Their handsomeness lay in the outer layers of skin, not in the fibres coming from within. They were surprised to see some people had faces covered with warts or spots, or otherwise disfigured. They said such faces were never to be seen among them. But they did approve of some faces, the ones that were cheerful and smiling, and had slightly pouting lips.

53. The reason why they approved of faces with pouting lips was that most of their speech consists of facial expressions, and it is particularly the region round the lips which they use. Also they never pretend, that is, they never say one thing and think another. So they do not force their faces but leave them free to express their thoughts. But those who have learned from childhood to pretend behave quite differently. They screw up their faces from within, to prevent any hint of what they think showing through. Nor does the outward part reveal anything, but they keep it ready to relax or screw up, as dictated by their cunning. The truth of this can be established by examining the fibres of the lips and the surrounding area. There are there manifold series of folded and connected fibres, designed not only for eating and speaking articulately, but also for expressing the ideas in the mind.

54. I was also shown how thoughts are expressed by means of the face. A person's looks display the affections his love produces and their changes; and variations in their inward form express thoughts. It is impossible to describe these more fully. The inhabitants of Jupiter also use verbal speech, but it does not sound so loud as ours. One way of speaking assists the other, and facial speech gives life to verbal speech.

(2) I was told by angels that the earliest kind of speech of all peoples on each world was by facial expression; and it originated from two areas, the lips and the eyes. The reason why this was the earliest form of speech was that the face was designed to portray what a person thinks and wants. The face is therefore called the picture and indicator of the mind. Another reason is that in the most ancient or earliest times honesty demanded that what a person

wanted should shine out from his face, and no one
thought of doing anything else or wanted to do so. Thus
too the affections of the mind and the thoughts arising
from them could be vividly and fully displayed. This enabled many things to be presented simultaneously to the
eye, as it were, in visible form. This kind of speech in consequence was as much better than verbal speech as sight is
better than hearing: the difference between seeing the
countryside and envisaging it by listening to a verbal
description.

They also said that this kind of speech matched the
speech of the angels, with whom human beings were in the
habit of communicating in those times. In fact, when the
face speaks, or the mind speaks through the face, angelic
speech reaches its final, natural form in a person; but not
when the mouth speaks in words. Anyone can grasp that
the most ancient people could not have had verbal speech,
since the words of language are not directly inherent in
things, but need to be invented and applied to them; and
this could only happen over a period of time.[23]

(3) This kind of speech lasted so long as honesty and
uprightness were observed by people. But as soon as people started to think one thing in their minds and say another, which happened when people began to love
themselves and not their neighbour, speech in words
began to increase, while the face conveyed nothing or told
lies. As a result the inward shape of the face changed, con-
tracting and hardening, and beginning to be almost devoid
of life. But its outward shape, fired by self-love, began to
look alive to men's eyes. For what lies hidden underneath
devoid of life is invisible to human eyes, but can be seen by
angels, who can see what lies within.

This is what the faces are like of those who think one

thing and say another. Pretence, hypocrisy, trickery and guile—which today pass for tactfulness—cause such results. But in the next life things are different; there you are not allowed to speak otherwise than you think. In fact, any disagreement is clearly perceptible in each single word; and when it is noticed the spirit who displays such disagreement is ejected from the company and punished. Afterwards various methods are applied to bring him back to speaking as he thinks and to thinking what he wants, so as to restore unanimity to his mind and banish division. The effect is, if he is good, that he wants what is good and thinks and speaks the truth as the result of good; if he is wicked, he wants what is evil and thinks and speaks falsely as the result of evil. Until this happens, a good man cannot be raised to heaven, nor a wicked one cast into hell. This is to ensure that hell contains nothing but wickedness and the falsity it produces, heaven nothing but good and the truth it produces.

55. I was further informed by the spirits from that world about various matters concerning its inhabitants, such as their way of moving, and their food and houses. When moving, they do not walk upright like the inhabitants of this and many other worlds; nor do they go on all fours like animals, but when they walk they help themselves with the flat of their hands, at every other pace half rising to their feet. As they move, at every third pace they turn their faces to one side and look behind them, making a slight twist, quickly accomplished, of the body. This is because they think it impolite to be seen by others except face to face.

(2) While they walk in this fashion, they always keep their faces up, as we do, so that they can see the sky as well

as the ground. They do not keep their gaze fixed on the ground, a practice they call reprehensible. The worst sort of people among them do this, and if they do not become used to lifting up their faces, they are banished from their community.

(3) When, however, they sit down, they look erect like people in our world as far as the upper part of the body is concerned, but they squat cross-legged. They take great care, not only when walking, but also when sitting, to avoid being seen from behind, but only in the face. In fact, they rather like to be seen face to face, since this displays their mind. They never display a facial expression which does not match their mind, something they find impossible. Those present can by this means see quite plainly what another's intentions towards them are, since they do not hide them, especially whether their apparent friendliness is genuine or forced. The spirits from there demonstrated this to me and their angels confirmed it. As a result their spirits too do not appear to walk upright, but rather like swimmers to assist their progress with their hands, looking around them from time to time.

56. Those of them who live in warm climates go naked apart from a loin-cloth; and they are not ashamed of their nakedness, because their minds are chaste, and they love none but their wives or husbands and loathe adultery. They were extremely surprised that the spirits of our world, on hearing that they walked like that and went naked, made fun of them and had lewd thoughts; also that they had no care for their life in heaven, but were only interested in matters of this kind. They said it was a sign that they care more for the things of the body and the earth than for those of heaven, and their minds are filled with improper thoughts. They told them that nakedness was no cause for embarrassment or scandal to those who live chastely in a state of innocence, but only to those who delight in lewdness and obscenity.

57. When the inhabitants of that world lie in their beds, they face forwards into the room, not backwards towards the wall. This was told me by their spirits, who gave the reason that they believe that by doing this they are facing the Lord, and turning their face away from Him if they turn their backs. Such an idea had several times occurred to me while I was in bed, but I did not know before from where it came.

58. They take great pleasure in protracted meals, not so much because they relish the food, as because of the pleasant conversation which accompanies it. When they sit down to eat, they do not sit on chairs or benches, or raised grassy banks, or even on the grass, but on the leaves of a certain tree. They would not tell me which tree the leaves were from, but when I guessed and named some, they finally said yes when I mentioned fig-leaves. They also said that they did not prepare their food to make it tasty, but more particularly with a view to its usefulness, remarking that useful food tastes good to them.

(2) There was some discussion about this among the spirits, and they said that this practice is suitable for human beings, for it is their heart's desire to have a healthy mind in a healthy body. But it is different for those who make taste the dominant factor. This makes the body ill, or at least internally languid, and this therefore has the same effect on the mind. The mind's behaviour depends on the inward condition of the receiving organs of the body, just as sight and hearing depend on the condition of the eye

and ear. It is therefore madness to make luxury and pleasure the whole joy of life; and it also leads to insensitivity in matters demanding thought, judgment and cleverness in matters relating to the body and the world. This results in human beings becoming like animals, and such people are not wrong in comparing themselves with them.

59. I was also shown their dwellings. They are low, built of wood, but lined inside with bark or cork of a light blue colour, studded all round and above with small stars to resemble the sky. They want to give their homes the appearance of the sky with its constellations. This is because they think of the constellations as the dwellings of angels. They also have tents with rounded tops and elongated in plan, these too studded with small stars inside on a blue background. They shelter in them during the day to prevent their faces getting sunburnt. They take a lot of trouble over making these tents and keeping them clean. They also use them for eating.

60. When the spirits of Jupiter saw the horses of this world, these looked to me smaller than usual, although they were quite strong and tall. This was due to the idea those spirits had of their own horses. They said that theirs were similar, but much bigger; they run wild in the forests and terrify them when they are sighted, though they do no harm. They also said they feel a naturally ingrained fear of them. This made me think about the cause of their fear. A horse in the spiritual sense means the intellectual faculty formed from factual knowledge[24]; and since they are afraid of developing this faculty by means of knowledge acquired from the world, this makes them afraid. As will be seen in what follows, they are not interested in the factual knowledge which constitutes human learning.

61. The spirits of that world are unwilling to associate with spirits from ours because of the difference in their character and behaviour. They call the spirits of our world cunning, quick and clever at devising evil, knowing or thinking little about good. Moreover the spirits of the world of Jupiter are much wiser than the spirits of our world. They say of ours that they talk too much and think too little, so that they cannot have much inward perception, even of what good is. From this they infer that the people of our world are external men.

(2) Some wicked spirits of our world were once permitted to exercise their wicked tricks so as to annoy the spirits from Jupiter who were with me. They put up with this for quite a long time, but eventually admitted they could stand no more. They could not believe that any worse spirits existed, for their imagination and thought were so perverted by these that they seemed as if tied up, with no hope of being untied and set free except by Divine aid. When I read some passages from the Word about our Saviour's passion, the European spirits introduced horrifying scandals, intending to corrupt the spirits of Jupiter. Enquiry was made into who they were and what they had been in the world. It turned out that some of them had been preachers, most of them from those who call themselves the Society of the Lord or Jesuits. I said that when they lived in the world they had been able to move the common people to tears by their preaching about the Lord's passion. The reason, I went on to say, was that in the world they thought one thing and said another, so differing in what they intended in their hearts and what they professed with their lips; but now they were not allowed to speak so deceitfully, for on becoming spirits they are compelled to speak as they think. The spirits from Jupiter were

particularly amazed that such a divorce between a person's interiors and exteriors was possible that they could say one thing and think another, something they found impossible.

(3) They were surprised to hear that many from our world actually become angels and were totally different at heart. They had supposed that all in our world were like the ones they had met. But they were told that many were not like that, and that there are those whose thoughts are dictated by goodness, not by wickedness as in the case of the others. These are the ones who become angels.

To show them this was true, choirs composed of angels from our world came from heaven, which one after another together glorified the Lord with one voice and in harmony.[25] The spirits of Jupiter with me were so charmed by these choirs they thought themselves almost carried up into heaven. This glorifying by choirs lasted about an hour, and the delight they felt in it was conveyed to me, so that I too could feel it. They said they would tell their friends who were not there about it.

62. The inhabitants of the world of Jupiter define wisdom as good and fair thinking about the events which happen in the course of living. This wisdom they absorb from their parents as children, and this is successively handed on to their descendants. The love of wisdom also contributes to it, since this increases when they become parents. They neither know nor wish to know anything about the sciences we have in our world. They call these shadows and liken them to the clouds which obscure* the sun. They formed this idea of the sciences from some spirits of our world, who boasted to them of the wisdom the sciences had given them.

---

* Reading *intercipiunt* for *inter*. —TR.

(2) The spirits from our world who made such boasts were those who regarded wisdom as merely a matter of memory, for instance, a knowledge of languages, particularly Hebrew, Greek and Latin, of experiences recorded in literature, of criticism, of experimental data, of technical terms, especially those of philosophy, and other things of the same sort. They had not used such knowledge as a means of acquiring wisdom, but regarded wisdom as consisting in the possession of such knowledge. Since they had not employed their knowledge as a means of improving their rational faculty, they have limited powers of perception in the next life. They can only discern technical terms and argue from them, and to those who see nothing else, such things are like dust or clouds obscuring the sight of the intellect (see §38 above). Those who were proud of this kind of learning are still less perceptive, while those who used their scientific knowledge as a means to undermine and annihilate the beliefs of the church have totally destroyed their intellectual faculty, so that their vision is like that of owls in pitch darkness, when they mistake falsity for truth and evil for good.

(3) Talking with such spirits made the spirits of Jupiter conclude that sciences produce obscurity and blindness. However, they were told that in this world sciences are the means of opening up the sight of the intellect, which depends on the light of heaven. But because of the dominance of matters concerned only with natural life, the life of the senses, these sciences serve them rather as means to madness, that is, proofs which favour Nature rather than God, and the world rather than heaven.

(4) They were further told that sciences are in themselves spiritual riches, and their possessors resemble the possessors of worldly riches; for these are likewise the

means of performing services to oneself, one's neighbour and one's country, and also the means of doing evil. They can also be compared with clothes, which are both useful and ornamental, and are also a matter of pride to those who want to be respected for them alone. The spirits of the world of Jupiter quite understood this, but they were surprised that, while still living as human beings, they had stopped at the means, and preferred the things which lead to wisdom to wisdom itself, failing to see that plunging the mind into means without rising beyond them is putting it in the shade and blinding it.

63. A certain spirit came up from the lower earth and approaching me said that he had heard my conversation with the other spirits, but had not understood the remarks about spiritual life and spiritual light. I asked whether he wanted to be taught about this, but he said that was not his intention in coming. I was able to infer from this that he would not be able to grasp such matters, being extremely stupid. The angels told me that while living in the world he had been among the more famous for their learning. He was cold, as could be plainly felt by the air around him. This was a sign of purely natural light with no spiritual light, so that he had not used his knowledge of the sciences to open up but to close off his path to the light of heaven.

64. Since the inhabitants of the world of Jupiter acquire intelligence in a different way from that of the inhabitants of our world, and have moreover by their manner of living acquired a different character, they cannot bear to be together for long, either moving away themselves or sending the others away. There are what we must call spiritual spheres continually emanating, or rather pouring out, from every spirit. Their source is the activity of their affections and the thoughts they produce, and so their life itself.[26] In the next life it is these spheres which determine association. Those which are harmonious bring spirits together so far as their harmony permits; those which are in conflict keep spirits apart as far as their conflict demands.

(2) The spirits and angels from the world of Jupiter answer to the PICTURING POWER OF THOUGHT in the Grand Man, that is, an activity of internal parts. The spirits of our world, however, answer to various functions of the external parts of the body. When these try to dominate, the activity or picturing of thought cannot exert its influence from within. This is the cause of the conflict between the life spheres of either party.

65. As regards their Divine worship, its principal tenet is the acknowledgment of our Lord as the Supreme Ruler of heaven and earth. They call Him the One and Only Lord. Since while living in the body they acknowledge and worship Him, they seek Him after death, and find Him; He is the same as our Lord. I asked them whether they knew that their One and Only Lord was a man. They answered that everyone knows He is a man, because many people on their planet have seen Him as a man. He teaches them about truth, preserves them, and confers everlasting life on those who out of goodness worship Him. They said further that He has revealed to them how they ought to live and what they ought to believe. This revelation is handed on from parents to children, so that the teaching spreads to all families, and thus to the whole tribe who have a single ancestor. They went on to say that it seems to them as if they had that teaching engraved on their minds. They reach this conclusion from the fact that they instantly perceive and acknowledge, as it were spontaneously, whether what others relate about a person's heavenly life is true or not.

(2) They do not know that their One and Only Lord was born as a man in our world. They remarked that this was of no interest to them, only that He was a man and the ruler of the universe. When I said that in our world He is called Christ Jesus, and that Christ means the Anointed or King, and Jesus Saviour, they said they do not worship Him as King, because kingship smacks of worldly affairs, but they do worship Him as Saviour. Some spirits from our world cast doubt on the identity of their Lord with ours; they dispelled this doubt by recalling that they had seen Him in the sun, and recognised Him as the one they had seen in their world (see §40 above).

(3) On another occasion spirits from Jupiter felt a momentary doubt of the identity of their One and Only Lord with ours. But the momentary doubt was dispelled in a moment; it was due to some spirits from our world. Then to my surprise they were so ashamed of having doubted this for a moment that they told me not to publish this, for fear of being accused of some degree of disbelief, though in fact they know this better than others.

(4) These spirits were very much affected and pleased when they were told that the One and Only Lord is the only man, and it is from Him that we all derive our humanity; that we are men to the extent that we are images of Him, in so far, that is, as we love Him and love our neighbour, so that we are in a state of good. For the goodness of love and faith is the image of the Lord.

66. Some spirits of the world of Jupiter were with me while I was reading Chapter 17 of JOHN, about the Lord's love and His glorification. On hearing what is written there, its holiness struck them and they admitted that everything there was Divine. But then some spirits of our world, who had been infidels, kept on suggesting scandalous ideas, saying that He was born as a baby, lived as a man, looked like any other man, was crucified and so forth. But the spirits of Jupiter paid no attention to these ideas. They said that these spirits resemble their devils, whom they loathed, adding that their minds were totally devoid of any heavenly element, being filled with earthy matter which they called slag. They said they had also learned that this was so, because on hearing that in their world they went naked, the thoughts of the spirits from our world immediately became lewd, and because they did not give any thought to their life in heaven, about which they had also then been told.

67. I was able to see plainly how clear a perception the spirits of Jupiter have about spiritual matters, by the way they pictured the Lord's method of turning wicked affections into good ones. They pictured the intellectual mind as a beautiful shape, and supplied it with activity matching the life of affection. They did this in a way indescribable in words, so cleverly as to excite praise from angels. There were present some learned men from our world, who had steeped their intellectual faculty in scientific terminology, writing and thinking much about form, substance, the material and the immaterial, and suchlike, without putting them to any use. These were unable to grasp even the representation of the idea as a picture.

68. In their world the greatest care is taken to prevent anyone falling into erroneous beliefs about the One and Only Lord. If they notice people beginning to think incorrectly about Him, they give them a warning, then threaten and finally punish them so as to make them desist. They said it had been their practice to get rid of any family so infected, not by sentence of death pronounced by their companions, but by spirits suppressing their breathing and so taking their lives, once they had first passed sentence of death on them. For in that world spirits talk with people and chastise them if they have done wrong, and also if they have formed the intention of doing so; I shall revert to this subject later. So if they have wrong thoughts about the One and Only Lord, they are sentenced to death, if they do not come to their senses. In this way the worship of the Lord, who is their supreme deity, is maintained.

69. They said that they kept no festivals, but every morning at sunrise and every evening at sunset they hold in their tents a service of holy worship of the One and Only Lord. They also sing their own kind of hymns.

70. I was further informed that in that world there are also some people who call themselves the Saints, and order their large numbers of servants on pain of punishment to address them as lords. They also forbid them to worship the Lord of the universe, saying that they are mediating lords, and that they will convey their prayers to the Lord of the universe. They do not, like the rest of the people there, call the Lord of the universe, who is our Lord, the One and Only Lord. They term Him the Most High Lord, because they call themselves lords.

(2) They call the sun of their world the face of the Most High Lord, and believe He has His dwelling there; for which reason they also worship the sun. The rest of the inhabitants loathe them, and will not have anything to do with them, both because they are sun-worshippers and be-

cause they call themselves lords, being adored by their servants as mediating deities.

(3) The spirits showed me the head-covering these people wore, which was a dark coloured top hat.

(4) In the next life they are to be seen to the left at some height, sitting there like statues, and to begin with adored by the servants they had had. But after a while these too treat them with ridicule. To my surprise their faces shine as if on fire; this is due to their belief in having been saints. But for all their fiery faces they are actually cold and desperately anxious to get warm. This makes it plain that the fire which makes them shine is the illusory fire of self-love. In order to get warm they seem to themselves to be sawing logs; while doing so, they catch sight beneath the logs of something like a man, whom they try at the same time to strike. This is the result of attributing merit and holiness to themselves. It is the fate of those who do this in this world to seem to saw logs in the next life. The same thing happened to some from our world too, whom I described elsewhere. As an illustration I may add here my experience with these people.

*"On the lower earth, beneath the soles of the feet are also those who regarded good deeds and works as meritorious. Many of them seem to themselves to be sawing logs. The place where they are is rather cold, and they seem to gain warmth by their work. I talked with them too, and was able to ask whether they did not wish to leave that place. They replied that they had not yet worked hard enough to deserve it. But on reaching the end of that stage they are released. They are natural men, because wanting

---

*The following paragraph is repeated with minor changes from *Arcana Coelestia* §4943.—Tr.

to earn salvation is not a spiritual idea, since it comes from the self, not from the Lord. Moreover they think themselves better than others, some of them actually despising others. If in the next life they do not receive more joy than the rest, they are angry with the Lord; as a result, when sawing logs, it looks to them as if something of the Lord is to be seen beneath the logs. This is the result of their indignation."27

71. It is a common event in that world for spirits to talk with its inhabitants, teaching them, and chastising them if they have misbehaved. Since I was told a great deal about this by their angels, I should like to report these experiences in order. The reason why spirits talk with people there is that they spend a lot of time thinking about heaven and life after death, and are relatively little concerned about life in the world. They know they will go on living when they die, and that the happiness of their state then depends upon the state of their internal man, which was formed in the world. Talking with spirits and angels was also a common event in this world in ancient times for the same reason: they thought much about heaven and little about the world. But in course of time that direct communication with heaven was cut off, as man became external instead of internal, or, which is the same thing, he began to think much about the world and little about heaven. This was even more the case when he no longer believed in the existence of heaven and hell, or in his possession of a personal spirit to live on after death. For at the present time the body is believed to have a life of its own instead of one coming from its spirit. If people therefore did not now have a belief in resurrection with a body, they would have no belief in resurrection at all.

72. As regards the presence of spirits with inhabitants of the world of Jupiter in detail, there are some spirits who chastise, some who instruct and some who control them. The chastising spirits attach themselves to the left side and lean towards the back; when in position, they draw out from a person's memory all he has done and thought. This is easy for spirits, since on approaching a person they can take over his whole memory.[9] If they find fault with his actions or thoughts, they reprove him and also chastise him by means of pains in the joints, the feet or the hands, or around the epigastric region. This is something spirits are very clever at doing, when permitted. When such spirits approach a person, they strike horror and fear into him, which makes him aware of their approach. Wicked spirits are able to inspire fear in a person when they approach, especially those who while living in the world were robbers.

(2) To allow me to know how these spirits behave on approaching a person of their world, one of them was permitted to approach me. When he was near, I had an unmistakable feeling of horror and fear, but it was an outward rather than inward horror, since I knew that he was a spirit of that kind. I could actually see him, looking like a dark cloud with moving stars in it. Moving stars indicate falsities, fixed stars truths.[20] He attached himself to my left side towards the back, and also began to reprove me for things I had done and thought, which he drew out of my memory, also putting a bad construction on them. But he was stopped by angels. On discovering that he was in the presence of someone other than a man of his own world, he began to talk with me, saying that on approaching a person he knew all the details of his deeds and thoughts, and he then uttered a severe reproof and chastised him with various sorts of pain.

(3) On another occasion too a similar chastising spirit visited me. He attached himself to me on the left side below the waist like the earlier one. He too wanted to punish me, but he was kept off by the angels. But he demonstrated to me the kinds of punishment they are allowed to inflict on people in their world, if they do or intend to do wicked deeds. Apart from the pain in the joints there was a painful contraction around the middle of the belly, which felt like being pulled in with a narrow belt; then another punishment was spells of choking until the victim was very distressed; also, preventing them eating anything but bread for a time; and finally a death sentence, if they failed to stop doing such things, and being deprived of the joys of wife, children and companions. These too were accompanied by a sensation of pain.

73. The instructing spirits also attach themselves to their left side, but more towards the front. They also reprove them, but mildly, and then teach them how they ought to live. These too appear dark, not like clouds as the previously mentioned ones, but as if dressed in sacks.

(2) They are called instructors, the others chastisers. When these spirits are present, angelic spirits are too. They sit by the head and fill it in their own manner. Their presence is felt like a gentle breath, for they are afraid of anyone suffering the slightest pain or anxiety at their approach or influence. They control the chastising and instructing spirits, making sure the one group does not do the person more harm than the Lord permits, and the other speaks the truth.

(3) When I had a chastising spirit with me, angelic spirits were then also present, keeping my face constantly cheerful and smiling, the region around my lips pushed

forward, and my mouth slightly open. Angels are easily able to do this by their influence, when the Lord permits. They said that their presence causes the inhabitants of their world to assume the same facial expression.

74. If after being chastised and instructed a person does evil again, or thinks of doing it, and fails to restrain himself in accordance with the commands of truth, then he is punished more severely when the chastising spirit returns. But angelic spirits temper his punishment, depending on the intention behind his acts and the will behind his thoughts. From this it might be deduced that their angels who sit by the head exercise some kind of judgment over the person, since they give permission, and exercise a moderating and restraining effect and influence. But I was told that it is not they who judge, but the Lord is the sole judge; all the commands given by the chastising and instructing spirits are inspired by His influence, in such a way that it seems to come from them.

75. In that world spirits talk with people, but they do not in turn talk with spirits. The only thing they say is, when instructed about something, that they will not do it any more. Nor are they allowed to tell anyone that a spirit has talked to them; if they do, they are afterwards punished. When the spirits of Jupiter were with me, they started by thinking they were with a man in their own world. But when I talked back to them, and also thought I should like to publish and tell others about my experiences, while they were not allowed to chastise and instruct me, they realised that they were with someone else.

76. There are two signals which these spirits receive when present with someone. They see an ancient man with a white face. This is a sign that they are not to speak anything but the truth or do anything but what is right. They also see a face in the window; this is a sign for them to leave. I too saw that ancient man, as well as the face in the window; as soon as it appeared, those spirits left me.

77. Apart from the spirits just mentioned, there are also spirits who offer the opposite advice. These are those who while living in the world were banished from the company of others on account of their wickedness. When they arrive, something like flying fire is seen falling close to the face. They station themselves to the rear of the person but below him, and speak upwards from that position. They say the opposite of what the instructing spirits conveyed from the angels; that one need not live as instructed, but one can please oneself and take liberties, and suchlike. They usually come after the previous spirits have left. But the people of that world know who these spirits are and what they are like, so they take no notice of them. But this is still a way of learning what evil is, and so what good is. Indeed, one can recognise the nature of goodness from its opposite. Everything is perceived by reflecting on its varying types and degrees of difference compared with its opposite.

78. The chastising and instructing spirits do not approach those who call themselves saints and mediating lords (see on these §70 above), as they do others in that world, because they are unwilling to be instructed and cannot be made better by discipline. They are incorrigible because they are motivated by self-love. The spirits said they recognise them by their coldness, and on feeling the cold they leave them.

79. Among the spirits of Jupiter there are some they call chimney-sweeps, because they dress like them and have a sooty face. I am allowed to describe who they are and what they are like. A spirit of this kind visited me and begged me insistently to intercede on his behalf, so that he could be admitted to heaven. He said he was unaware of having done evil; he had only criticised the inhabitants of his world, adding that after criticising them he had instructed them. He attached himself to my left side below the elbow; and he spoke as it were with a forked tongue. He might well have inspired pity; but I could only reply to him that I could not give him any help, since this was the Lord's alone to give. Nor could I intercede, not knowing whether it was any use or not. But if he deserved it, I told him he could hope. He was then sent back to join the upright spirits from his world. But they said that his nature made it impossible for him to be in their company. However, since he was so keen that he kept begging to be admitted to heaven, he was sent to a community of upright spirits from this world. But they too said he could not stay with them. He appeared black in the light of heaven, though he claimed himself not to be black, but a reddish brown colour.

(2) I was told that the spirits are like this to begin with who are subsequently found a home among those who make up the province of the SEMINAL VESICLES in the Grand Man or heaven. The semen gathers in those vesicles and is clothed in material suitable for preserving the prolific principle of the semen from being dissipated; but this can be shed at the cervix of the uterus, so that what is contained within can serve the purpose of causing conception, that is, of impregnating the ovum. As a result this part of the semen displays an effort and as it were a burning desire

to strip itself off, leaving the semen to perform its function. Something similar was to be seen in the case of this spirit. He came to me in rough clothing and repeated that he was burning with desire to reach heaven, and he now began to perceive that he was the kind of spirit who could. I was allowed to tell him that this was perhaps an indication that he would soon be admitted. He was then told by angels to take off his clothes; he was so eager that he got them off quicker than anything. This was a way of picturing the nature of the desire of those in the province answering to the seminal vesicles.

(3) I was told that such spirits, when prepared for heaven, are stripped of their clothes and dressed in shining new ones, and they become angels. They likened them to grubs, which after passing through their humble stage are changed into nymphs and so into butterflies; these then receive a different dress with wings of blue, yellow, silvery or golden colour. Then they are free to fly in the air, as if their own heaven, celebrate marriages and lay eggs, thus ensuring the propagation of their kind. Then at the same time they are assigned as food the sweet and pleasant nectar and fragrance of various flowers.

80. I have not said in what I have written so far what the angels from that world are like. Those who visit people in their world and sit by their heads (see §73 above) are not angels in their inner heaven, but angelic spirits or angels in their outer heaven. Since the nature of these angels has been disclosed to me, I should like to report what I was allowed to learn about them.

(2) One of the spirits of Jupiter who inspire fear came up to my left side below the elbow and talked with me from that position. His speech was strident, nor were the

words separate and divided one from another, so that it took a long time before I was able to grasp his meaning. While he was speaking, he also struck fear into me at times. He warned me that I too should make the angels welcome when they came. But I was allowed to answer that it was not for me to do this, but all were received in my presence as they are themselves.

(3) Soon some angels from that world arrived, and I was able to perceive from the way they talked with me that they were quite different from the angels of our world. Their speech was not in spoken words, but in ideas which spread in all directions through my interiors; they also had an effect on my face, making it agree with each detail, beginning from the lips and spreading out to the periphery in all directions. The ideas which took the place of words were separated, but only slightly.

(4) Afterwards they talked with me by means of ideas even less separate one from another, so that there seemed to be hardly any interval between them. It seemed to my way of perception like the sense of words apprehended by those who pay attention to the sense but ignore the words. I found this speech easier to understand, and more filled with meaning. Like the previous kind of speech its influence was felt on the face, but to match their speech this was more continuous. But unlike the previous kind it did not begin from the lips, but from the eyes.

(5) Later still they spoke even more continuously and fully, and then my face was unable to keep pace with suitable movements; but I felt the influence acting on my brain, which then behaved in similar fashion. Finally they spoke in such a way that their speech fell only on my inner intellect. It was as fluid as a rarefied atmosphere. I could feel the influence, but not distinguish its details.

These types of speech were rather like fluids; the first like flowing water, the second like a more rarefied liquid, the third in comparison like air, and the fourth like a rarefied atmosphere. The spirit on my left side, whom I mentioned before, interjected remarks from time to time, especially to warn me to show restraint in dealing with his angels. For there were spirits from our world who introduced unpleasant ideas. He said he had not understood what the angels were saying, but he did later on, when he came close to my left ear. At that time too his speech was not as strident as before, but like that of other spirits.

81. Later I talked with the angels about experiences in our world, especially about printing here, the Word and various of the church's teachings drawn from the Word. I told them that the Word and religious teachings are published and so disseminated. They were very surprised that such matters could be published by books and printing.

82. I was allowed to see what happens when spirits from that world are, once prepared, carried off to heaven and become angels. At these times chariots and horses are seen shining as if on fire, like those which carried off Elijah. The appearance of chariots and horses shining as if on fire is because this is a picture of their being instructed and prepared for entering heaven. Chariots mean the teaching of the church, and shining horses the enlightened intellect.[28]

83. The heaven into which they are taken is to be seen to the right of their world, so separated from the heaven of angels from our world. The angels in that heaven appear dressed in bright blue studded with small gold stars. This is because they were fond of that colour while in the world. They also believed it to be the most heavenly colour, especially because they are in a state of good of love corresponding to that colour.[29]

84. I saw a bald head, but only its upper, bony part; and I was told that those who are due to die within a year see such a vision, and they then prepare themselves. The people there are not afraid of dying, apart from having to leave their wife, children or parents, because they know they will go on living after death. They know they are not leaving life, because they are going to heaven; so they do not call it dying, but becoming heavenly. If in that world they have lived in a state of truly conjugial love and have taken care of their children as parents should, they do not die of disease, but peacefully as if in sleep; and so they pass from that world to heaven.

(2) The average age of people there at death is thirty, counting by the years of this world. The reason why they die within such a short span of time is that the Lord's Providence ensures that the population does not exceed the numbers who can be supported by that world. It is also because after reaching that age, they resist the guidance of spirits and angels, which those who have not yet reached that age accept, so that spirits and angels rarely approach those who are older. They reach maturity more quickly than people in our world, and get married in the first flush of youth. Their delights then are to love their wife or husband, and to take care of their children. Their other delights they admittedly call delights, but comparatively external ones.

The World or Planet of Mars, and Its Spirits and Inhabitants

85. The spirits of Mars are among the best of all spirits from the worlds of this solar system. For to a large extent they are like celestial men, not dissimilar from those of the Most Ancient Church in this world.[30] When their nature is pictured, they are shown with their faces in heaven and their bodies in the world of spirits, and those of them who are angels with their faces turned towards the Lord, and their bodies in heaven.

86. The planet Mars is thought of by spirits and angels as occupying a fixed position, as the other planets do; this lies in front to the left, some distance away at chest level, that is to say, outside the sphere where the spirits of our world are. The spirits of one world are separated from those of another, because the spirits of each world answer to some particular province in the Grand Man.[6] As a result their states are not the same but diverse, and this diversity of state makes them appear separated from one another, either to the right or to the left, and at a greater or lesser distance.[31]

87. Some spirits came to me from there and attached themselves to my left temple. There they breathed speech over me, but I did not understand it. Its flow was extremely gentle; I had never felt anything so gentle, like the gentlest of breezes. It first blew upon my left temple and my left ear from above; then it proceeded to my left eye, moving gradually to the right and then flowing down, especially from the left eye, to the lips. On reaching the lips, it entered the mouth, and travelling through the mouth proceeded, in fact through the Eustachian tube, into the brain. When the breath reached that point, I understood their speech and was able to talk with them. I noticed that when they were talking with me, my lips moved and to a small extent my tongue did also. This was due to the correspondence between inward and outward speech. Outward speech consists of articulate sounds travelling to the outer membrane of the ear, and then by means of small organs, membranes and fibres inside the ear being carried to the brain.

(2) It may be known from this that the speech of the inhabitants of Mars is of a different type from that of the inhabitants of our world. It has little sound, but is almost silent, following a shorter path to penetrate the inner hearing and sight. Being of such a nature it is more perfect, more full of the concepts of thought, and so closer to the speech of spirits and angels. The actual affection in the speech is pictured in their faces, and the thought in their

eyes; for with them thought and speech, as well as affection
and facial expression, act as one. They consider it a crime
to think one thing and say another, or to wish for one
thing and show something else by facial expression. They
do not know what hypocrisy or deceitful pretence or
guile are.

(3) I have been able to learn by associating with certain
of the Most Ancient peoples of this world that they too
could speak like this. To illustrate this I should like to report what I have heard, as follows.

*"I was shown by a kind of influence which I cannot
describe what speech was like among those who belonged
to the Most Ancient Church.[30] It was not articulate, as
speech in words is in our time, but silent. It was produced
not by outer breathing, but by a kind of inner breathing,
so it might be termed thought-speech. I was also able to
grasp what inner breathing was like; it proceeded from the
navel towards the heart, and so through the lips without
making any sound when they spoke. It did not enter the
other's ear by the external route, striking on what is called
the eardrum, but by an internal route, in fact by what is
nowadays called the Eustachian tube. I was shown how by
speaking like this they could express much more fully the
decisions of the mind and the ideas of thought than can
ever be achieved by articulate sounds or spoken words.
Such speech is equally regulated by breathing, but this is
outer breathing. For there is no word, or rather no part of
a word, which is not regulated by the expiration of breath.
But in the case of these people it was much more perfect,
because it was regulated by inner breathing, which,

* The following paragraph is repeated with some changes from *Arcana
Coelestia* §1118.—Tr.

because it is internal is more perfect, and better suited and adapted to the ideas of thought. Moreover it was helped by slight movements of the lips and corresponding changes of facial expression. For, since they were celestial people, whatever they thought shone out from their faces and eyes. These changed in conformity, the facial expression reflecting the affections of their lives, the eyes the light. They were never able to display a look on their faces which did not agree with what they were thinking. Since they spoke by means of inner breathing, the breathing of a person's very spirit, they were able to associate and talk with angels."

(4) The way the spirits of Mars breathed was demonstrated to me,[32] and I perceived that their breathing proceeded from the region of the thorax towards the navel, and from there flowed up through the chest towards the mouth with an imperceptible expiration. This, together with the other proofs I experienced, allowed me to see that they possessed a celestial character, so that they were not dissimilar from those who belonged to the Most Ancient Church in this world.

88. I was informed that the spirits of Mars answer in the Grand Man to the middle term between the intellectual and the voluntary, that is, THINKING BASED UPON AFFECTION, and in the best of them THE AFFECTION OF THOUGHT. That is why their faces act as one with their thought, and they are unable to pretend to anyone. Since this is what they answer to in the Grand Man, the middle province between the cerebrum and the cerebellum corresponds to them. For those who have their cerebrum and their cerebellum linked as regards spiritual functions have their faces acting in unison with their thinking, so that the actual affection of their thought shines out from their faces, and the general drift of their thinking resulting from their affection is displayed by signs which also proceed from the eyes. For this reason while they were with me, I could definitely feel the fore part of my head being pulled towards the back of the head, that is to say, the cerebrum being pulled towards the cerebellum.[33]

89. On one occasion when the spirits of Mars were with me and had taken over the sphere in which my mind operates, some spirits from our world arrived and wanted to make their way into the same sphere. But this caused the spirits of our world to go mad, because they were totally unsuited to it. The spirits of our world answer in the Grand Man to external sense, so that their ideas were directed towards the world and themselves, but those of Mars had their ideas directed towards heaven and the neighbour. This was the cause of the conflict. But then angelic spirits of Mars arrived, who by their arrival broke off communication, so that the spirits of our world departed.

90. The angelic spirits talked with me about how the inhabitants of their world lived. They are not, they said, subjects of kingdoms, but divided into larger and smaller communities, in which they associate those of like character with themselves. They know this instantly from their faces and their speech, and rarely make any mistake about it; so they become friends at once. They also said that they take great pleasure in their meetings, at which they discuss what goes on in their communities; and especially what goes on in heaven, for many of them enjoy open communication with the angels of heaven.

(2) Any in their communities who begin to have wrong thoughts, leading to evil intentions, are banished

from them. They leave them by themselves, so that they live pitifully outside their community, among rocks or elsewhere, being no longer looked after by it. Some communities try various methods of bringing them to their senses; but when these attempts prove vain they break off contact with them. By such means they take precautions to prevent the desire to rule or to gain wealth sneaking in; that is to say, they make sure that no one out of a desire to rule gets control of one community, and then many more, and that no one out of a desire for wealth steals their property from others. Each individual there lives content with his own property, and with his own good name, a reputation for being fair and loving his neighbour. This pleasure and peace of mind would be destroyed, if those who think and intend evil were not ejected, and if they did not prudently and severely confront self-love and the love of the world in their earliest stages. It is these loves which are the motives behind empires and kingdoms. In these there are few who do not want to rule and possess other people's property, for there are few who behave justly and fairly from a love of justice and fairness, even fewer who do good out of charity rather than through fear of the law or being deprived of their lives, of wealth, or of good name and reputation for that reason.

91. On the subject of Divine worship by the inhabitants of that world they said that they acknowledge and worship our Lord, calling Him the Only God, and the ruler of heaven and the universe; all good comes from Him, and He guides them. He is often to be seen by them in their world. I was then able to tell them that Christians in our world too know that the Lord is the ruler of heaven and earth from the Lord's own words in Matthew:

> All power has been given to me in heaven and on
> earth. (Matt. 28:18)

But unlike those from the world of Mars, Christians do
not believe this.

(2) They also said that they have a belief there, that
there is nothing about them which is not filthy and hellish,
and that all good is the Lord's. Indeed they went so far as
to say that of themselves they are devils, and the Lord res-
cues them from hell, continually holding them back.

(3) Once when the Lord was named, I saw those spirits abase themselves so sincerely and deeply that I cannot
describe it. Their self-abasement contained the thought
that of themselves they were in hell, so that they were utterly unworthy of looking towards the Lord, who is holiness itself. This thought was so deeply planted in their
belief that they were almost beside themselves, and it kept
them on their knees until the Lord lifted them up, and
then, as it were, rescued them from hell. On recovering
from this self-abasement they are filled with good and love,
which gives them heartfelt joy. When they abase themselves like this, they do not face towards the Lord, not dar-
ing to do so, but look away. The spirits who were around
me said that they had never witnessed such self-abasement.

92. Some of the spirits from that world were surprised
that I was surrounded by so many spirits from hell, and
that they too talked to me. But I was able to reply that
they had this permission to enable me to know what they
were like and why they were in hell, in fact, that this was
the result of the life they had led. I was also able to say that
there were many among them whom I had known during
their lives in the world, some of them then holding high
rank, but counting nothing dear but the world. I assured

them that no wicked spirit, even the most hellish of them, could ever do me an injury, because I was constantly protected by the Lord.

93. One of the inhabitants of that world was shown to me, or rather, not an actual inhabitant, but a spirit who resembled one. His face was like that of the inhabitants of our world, but the lower part of his face was black, not with a beard, for he had none, but due to a black area taking its place. This blackness extended up under his ears on either side. The upper part of his face was sallow, like the faces of people in our world who are not completely white.

They went on to say that the food eaten in that world is the fruit of trees, especially a certain round fruit which grows on their earth, and also vegetables. Their clothing consists of garments which they make out of the bark fibres of certain trees. These have such a consistency that they can be woven and also glued together with a kind of gum they have. Moreover they reported that they know there how to make liquid fires, to provide themselves with light in the evening and at night.

94. I saw a most beautiful flaming object, of varying colour, purple then changing from white to red. The flame gave the colours a most beautiful reddish tinge. I also saw a hand to which this flaming object adhered, at first to the back of the hand, then to the palm or hollow of the hand, from where it licked all round. This lasted for some time; then the hand together with the flaming object moved off to a distance, and filled the place where it stopped with light. The hand receded in this bright area, and then the flaming object turned into a bird. To begin with the bird had the same colours as the flame and its colours glittered in the same way, but then they underwent a series of changes, and as they changed, so did the bird's liveliness. It flew around, first round my head, then ahead of me into a narrow room which resembled a shrine. The further it flew ahead, the more its liveliness declined, until at last it was turned to stone. At first its colour was like pearl, but later dark; and for all that it was lifeless, it could still fly.

(2) While this bird was flying round my head and was still lively, a spirit was seen rising up from below through the region of the loins as far as the chest. He wanted to take the bird away, but because it was so beautiful, the spirits around me prevented him, for they all had their gaze fixed on it. But the spirit who had come up insistently persuaded them that he had the Lord with him, and was acting on His instructions. Although most of them did not believe this, they stopped preventing him from taking away the bird. But at that instant an influence from heaven forced him to let go, and he quickly let it fly free from his hand.

(3) After this incident the spirits around me, who had watched the bird and its successive changes intently, discussed it among themselves for quite a long time. They perceived that such a vision must certainly have some heavenly meaning. They knew that something flaming means celestial love and its affections; the hand to which it adhered means life and the power of life; the changes of colour, variations in life as regards wisdom and intelligence. A bird has a similar meaning, with the difference that something flaming means celestial love and what is to do with it, a bird spiritual love and what is to do with that. (Celestial love is love to the Lord, spiritual love is charity towards the neighbour.)[30] The bird's changes in colour and liveliness, until it was turned to stone, mean successive changes in spiritual life as regards intelligence.

(4) They also knew that spirits who come up through the region of the loins to that of the chest cling obstinately to the false belief that they are in the Lord, so that they believe that everything they do, however wicked, is done with the Lord's consent. However, this was not enough to let them know who it was that were meant by this vision. They were eventually informed from heaven that the inhabitants of Mars were meant. Their celestial love, which many of them still retain, was meant by the flaming object which adhered to the hand. The bird to begin with, when its colours were at their loveliest and its liveliness most vigorous, meant their spiritual love. However, when the bird was turned to stone and became lifeless, eventually turning a dark colour, this meant the inhabitants of that world who departed from the good of love and are devoted to evil, while still believing that they are in the Lord. The spirit who rose up and wanted to carry off the bird had a similar meaning.

95. The stone bird was also a representation of the inhabitants of that world who in a strange manner transform the thoughts and affections of their life into one which hardly exists. I heard the following said on this subject.

(2) There was a spirit over my head who talked with me. It was possible to tell from the sound of his voice that he was more or less in a sleeping state. In this he talked a lot, and displayed such prudence in what he said that he could not have done better wide awake. I was able to perceive that he was being used as a person through whom angels spoke; in that state he could grasp what was said and reproduce it.[34] For he spoke nothing but the truth, and if he felt any influence from another source, he allowed it in, but did not reproduce it. I asked him about his state, and

he said that it was one of peace, and he had no anxiety about the future. At the same time he provided services, which allowed him to be in touch with heaven. I was told that such people answer in the Grand Man to the superior sagittal sinus, which lies between the two hemispheres of the brain, and they remain in a quiet condition there, however much the brain on either side is in turmoil.

(3) While I was talking with this spirit, some spirits moved towards the fore part of the head, where the one was whom they were crowding out. He therefore went off to one side to make room for them. These spirit newcomers were talking among themselves, but neither I nor the spirits around me could understand what they were saying. I was informed by angels that they were spirits from the world of Mars, who possessed the trick of talking among themselves without the other spirits present understanding or perceiving anything. I was surprised that such speech was possible, since all spirits share a common language, which flows from their thought, and is composed of ideas, which are heard as words in the spiritual world. I was told that those spirits have a special way of forming ideas, which they express by means of the lips and face, so that others cannot understand them; and at the same moment they deliberately withdraw their thoughts, taking particular care to allow no hint of their affection to show. This is because, if any hint of affection were perceived, then the thought would be obvious, since thought flows from the affection and is, as it were, contained in it.

I was informed further that the inhabitants of the world of Mars, not however all of them, but those who regard heavenly life as merely a matter of knowledge, not of showing love in the way they live, have devised this way of speaking, and on becoming spirits they retain this. It is these who are especially meant by the stone bird. For producing speech by means of facial expressions and convolutions of the lips, while removing affections and withdrawing thoughts from others, is taking the life out of speech and making it like a statue, and gradually making oneself like one too.

(4) But although they fancy that their conversations among themselves are not intelligible to others, still angelic spirits perceive all the details of their conversations. This is because not all the thought behind them can be withdrawn. To prove this to them they were given a live demonstration. I was pondering the fact that the wicked spirits of our world are not ashamed of attacking others. This idea reached me from angelic spirits who perceived their speech. Those Martian spirits then acknowledged, to their own surprise, that this was the subject of their conversation. Moreover, an angelic spirit was able to uncover more of their conversations and thoughts, however hard they tried to withdraw their thoughts from him.

(5) Later these spirits exercised an influence from above on my face. It looked like a fine striped rain; this was a sign that they had no affection for truth and good, for this is pictured by stripes. Then they spoke openly with me, and said that the inhabitants of their world converse in a similar manner. They were told that this was wicked, because it blocks off the internals, so that they leave these for the externals, and they deprive them too of life. It is particularly wicked because speaking like that is dishonest. Honest people have no wish to say or even think anything which others may not know, even if the others include everyone, even the whole of heaven. But those who do not want others to know what they say are passing judgment on others, holding a poor opinion of them and a good one

of themselves; and the habit reduces them to the point that they hold and express a poor opinion of the church, heaven and even the Lord Himself.

(6) I was told that those who love knowledge, without living as knowledge dictates, answer in the Grand Man to the inner membrane of the skull. But those who have become accustomed to speak without affection and to keep their thoughts to themselves, not sharing them with others, answer to that membrane when ossified, because from having some spiritual life they come to have none.

96. Since the stone bird also presented a picture of those who are only interested in what they know, and lack any life of love, and consequently any spiritual life, I should like to add here as a note a demonstration that only those who possess heavenly love, and have that as the source of their knowledge, have spiritual life. I will also show that a love contains in itself all the knowledge needed by that love.

Take as an example the animals of the earth, and also the creatures of the sky, the birds. They know everything needed by their loves. These loves are: to feed themselves, to find a safe place to live, to reproduce, to bring up their young, in some cases to build up a store for the winter. They have therefore all the knowledge they need, since this is contained in these loves and is imparted to them, as if to receptors designed for the purpose. In the case of certain animals this knowledge is such as to cause us profound astonishment. Their knowledge is inborn, and we call it instinct, but it belongs to the natural love which is theirs.

(2) If man possessed his proper love, love to God and towards the neighbour (this is man's proper love, a heavenly love distinguishing him from the beasts), then man would have not only all the knowledge he needs, but also

all intelligence and wisdom; for these flow into those loves from heaven, that is, from the Deity by way of heaven. But because man does not acquire those loves by birth, but their opposites, self-love and the love of the world, he cannot help acquiring by birth all ignorance and lack of knowledge. Yet by Divine means he is led towards some degree of intelligence and wisdom, though he does not actually acquire any, unless self-love and the love of the world are taken away, thus opening the way to love to God and towards the neighbour.

(3) Love to God and love towards the neighbour contain in themselves all intelligence and wisdom, as may be proved by those who possessed those loves in the world. On coming after death into heaven they have there such knoweldge and wisdom as they were previously quite unaware of. In fact, they think and talk there like the rest of the angels, saying ineffable things, which their ears had never heard nor their minds known. The reason is that these loves possess the ability to receive such things into themselves.

On the World or Planet of Saturn, and Its Spirits and Inhabitants

97. The spirits from that world are to be seen in front at a considerable distance, lower down on a level with the knees; and this is where that world too appears. When the gaze is turned in that direction, a great number of spirits, all from that world, comes into view. They are to be seen on this side of that world, and to the right of it. I was allowed to talk with them too, and so to discover what they are like as compared with others. They are upright and restrained; and because they have a low opinion of themselves, they also appear small in the next life.

98. They are very humble in their worship, for they regard themselves as worthless in this respect. They worship our Lord, and acknowledge Him as the One and Only God. The Lord actually appears to them from time to time in the form of an angel, that is, as a man; and then His Divinity shines out from His face, and affects their minds. The inhabitants also speak with spirits, when they are old enough; the spirits teach them about the Lord, how He should be worshipped, and how they ought to live.

Whenever anyone wants to mislead the spirits from there, seducing them from their belief in the Lord, or from their self-abasement before Him and from uprightness of life, they say they want to die. Then there are to be seen in their hands small knives, with which they seem intent on striking their chests. On being asked why they do this, they reply that they would rather die than be taken away from the Lord. The spirits of our world sometimes make fun of them on this account, and heap insults on them for behaving like that. But then they reply that they are perfectly well aware that they are not killing themselves, but that this is merely an appearance arising from their intention, which makes them prefer death to being prevented from worshipping the Lord.

99. They related that sometimes they are visited by spirits from our world, who ask them what God they worship. Their reply is that their questioners must be mad, and there can be no greater madness than to ask what God anyone worships, seeing that there is one sole God for all in the universe; and it is even more madness not to say that the Lord is that sole God, who controls the whole heaven and so the whole world. For the controller of heaven is also the controller of the world, since the world is controlled by means of heaven.

100. They said there were some people in their world who call their nocturnal luminary, which is vast, the Lord. But these are kept apart from the rest and are not tolerated by them. Their nocturnal illumination comes from the great ring which surrounds their world at a distance, and from the moons we know as the satellites of Saturn.

101. They reported that spirits of another kind, who travel in squadrons, often visit them, desiring to know how things are with them. They have various ways of finding out from them what they know. They said of these that they are not mad, except only in that they are so keen on knowledge for no other purpose than that of acquiring it. Later they were informed that these spirits came from the planet Mercury, that is, from the world nearest the sun, and they take pleasure only in what they know, not so much in the use to which it can be put.

102. The inhabitants and spirits of the planet Saturn answer in the Grand Man to the *sense which is midway between the spiritual and the natural man,* but which departs from the natural and verges on the spiritual. This is why those spirits are seen to be carried off or hurried into heaven, and then shortly to be sent back. For anything to do with spiritual sense is in heaven, but anything to do with natural sense is below heaven.

(2) Since the spirits of our world answer in the Grand Man to natural and bodily sense, I have been allowed to learn by plain experience how the spiritual and the natural man fight and quarrel, if the natural man is not in a state of faith and charity.

(3) The spirits of the world of Saturn were seen coming from far off, and then direct communication was established between them and such spirits of our world. On becoming aware of them our spirits became almost mad, and started to attack them, throwing out disparaging remarks about faith and also about the Lord; and amid their

rudeness and insults they actually plunged in among them, and the madness from which they were suffering made them attempt to inflict injury. But the spirits of Saturn were not at all frightened, being safe and calm. However, the spirits of our world, finding themselves among them. began to be distressed and to have difficulty in breathing, so that they hurled themselves away, one in one direction, another in another, and disappeared.

(4) This made the bystanders aware what the natural man is like, if he is separated from the spiritual man, when he enters a spiritual sphere; he is driven mad. For the natural man when separated from the spiritual can draw only on the world's wisdom, and gets nothing from heaven. Anyone who relies only on the world's wisdom believes nothing but what his senses tell him, and trusts what the deceptive impressions of the senses make him believe. Unless these are taken away by influence from the spiritual world, they lead to false beliefs. That is why spiritual matters are meaningless to him, to such a point that he can scarcely bear to hear the spiritual mentioned. As a result such people go mad, if they are kept in a spiritual sphere. But this does not happen while they are living in the world. Then they either think about spiritual matters in a natural way, or they close their ears to them, that is, they hear but do not listen.

(5) That experience also proved that the natural man cannot invade, that is, climb up to, the spiritual man. But when a person is in a state of faith and thus enjoys spiritual life, the spiritual man exerts an influence on the natural man, and thinks in him. Spiritual influence, that is, an influence from the spiritual world, can occur working on the natural world, but not the reverse.[35]

103. I was given further information by the spirits of that world about its inhabitants, revealing amongst other things the nature of their society. They said that they live grouped into families, each one separate from others. So a husband and wife with their children form a group. When the children marry, they leave their parents' home and take no further interest in it. As a result the spirits of that world are to be seen in pairs. They do not bother much about food and clothing. They live on the fruits and vegetables their world produces. They wear light clothing, since they are protected by a thick skin or coating, which keeps out the cold. Moreover, they told me that all the people in their world know that they will live on after death, so they pay no attention to their bodies, except so far as to keep alive. Life they say will continue, and will be devoted to the Lord's service. It is for the same reason too they do not bury the bodies of the dead, but throw them out, covering them with branches from the trees of the forest.

104. When I asked about the great ring which can be seen from our planet to rise above the horizon of that planet, and to change its aspect, they said that they did not see it as a ring, but only as a whiteness in the sky in various directions.

On the World or Planet of Venus, and Its Spirits and Inhabitants

105. Spirits and angels think of the planet Venus as to be seen on the left, a little further back and at some distance from our world. I say that the spirits think of it like this, because the sun of the solar system is not visible to any spirit, nor is any planet. Spirits simply have an idea of their existence. This idea alone makes them think of the sun of the solar system as something jet-black behind them, and the planets not wandering as in the solar system, but occupying fixed positions (see §42 above).

106. There are two kinds of people on the planet Venus, who are of opposite characters. Some are gentle and humane, some are fierce and almost like wild animals. Those who are gentle and humane are to be seen on the other side of their world; those who are fierce and almost like wild animals on the side facing us. It must be appreciated that this appearance is dependent on the way they live, because it is this which causes all apparent space and distance in that world.

107. Some of those who are to be seen on the other side of the planet, those who are gentle and humane, came to visit me; they came into view above my head and I had conversations with them on various subjects. Amongst other things they said that when they were in the world they had acknowledged, and now did so more than ever, our Lord as their one and only God. They declared that they had seen Him in their world, and pictured to me how He had appeared to them. These spirits answer in the Grand Man to *the memory of material things which is in agreement with the memory of immaterial things;* this last is what the spirits of Mercury answer to. As a result the spirits of Mercury are very much in harmony with these spirits from Venus. So when they were together, the influence from them provoked a notable change and strong action on my brain (see §43 above).

108. I did not, however, talk with the spirits on the side facing us, who are fierce and almost like wild animals; but the angels told me about their nature and the source of their wildness. They said that they took great pleasure in stealing, and particularly in eating what they had stolen. Their pleasure in this, when they were thinking of eating what they had stolen, was imparted to me, and I could grasp how overpowering it was. There were once people in our world who had a similarly wild nature, as is plain from the histories of various peoples; also from the inhabitants of the land of Canaan (1 Sam. 30:16). This also appears from the Jewish and Israelite people in the time of David, when they made raids every year to take booty from other peoples, and feasted gleefully on the spoil. I was also told that these inhabitants are for the most part giants, and people of our world only come up to their navel. Furthermore they are stupid and do not ask what heaven is or everlasting [life]*, but care only for what concerns their lands and their flocks.

109. Being of such a nature, when they come into the next life, they are there attacked most severely by evils and falsities. Their hells are to be seen near their world, and have no contact with the hells of the wicked from our world. This is because they are utterly different in nature and character, so that their evils and falsities are of a totally different type.

110. However, those of them who are such as can be saved are in places of vastation, where they are reduced to the uttermost despair. There is no other way that evils and falsities of that sort can be subdued and taken away. When they are in a state of desperation, they cry out that they are beasts, abominations, hateful, and therefore damned. When in that state, some of them even cry out against heaven; but they are forgiven for this because it is due to their despair. The Lord restrains them from going beyond fixed limits in calling down curses. After extremes of suffering, because their bodily parts are virtually dead, these are eventually saved. I was also told that, when these people lived in their world, they believed in some supreme

---

*Restored from *Arcana Coelestia* §7249.—TR.

Creator without any Mediator; but when saved, they are taught that the Lord is alone God, Saviour and Mediator. I saw some of them after extremes of suffering taken up into heaven; and when they were received there, I felt such a happy tenderness as to wring tears from my eyes.

On the Spirits and Inhabitants of the Moon

111. Some spirits appeared overhead, and I heard from there voices like thunder; for their voices thundered just like the claps of thunder which come from the clouds following lightning flashes. I supposed that there were a huge number of spirits who knew the trick of making their voices sound like that. The more simple spirits present with me laughed at them, which very much surprised me. The reason for their laughter was soon revealed, which was that these thundering spirits were not numerous, but only few, and also as small as boys. Another reason was that previously they had struck terror into them by similar thunderings, yet had not been able to do them any harm.

(2) To show me what they were like, some of them

came down from the height where they were thundering. I was surprised to see one carrying another on his back, so they approached me as a pair. Their faces were not unattractive in appearance, but longer than those of other spirits. In height they resembled a boy of seven, but were stronger in body; so they were dwarfs. I was told by angels that they were from the moon.

(3) The one who was carried by another came to me, attaching himself to my left side below the elbow. He spoke to me from that position, and said that when they give voice they thunder like that. This frightens spirits who want to harm them, making some of them run away, so that they can go where they want in safety. To prove to me that they could make such a noise, he retreated from me to join a few others, but without going out of sight, and made the same kind of thunder. Moreover, they demonstrated that their voice came out of their abdomen like a belch, and this caused the thunder.

(4) I gathered that this arises from the fact that the inhabitants of the moon do not speak so much from the lungs like the inhabitants of other worlds, but from the abdomen, using some air which collects there. This is because the moon is not surrounded by the same kind of atmosphere as the other worlds. I was informed that the spirits of the moon answer in the Grand Man to the scutiform or xiphoid cartilage*, to which the ribs are connected in front, and from which the *linea alba* descends, which is the fulcrum of the abdominal muscles.

---

*Both these terms were formerly in use for what is today generally called the sternum.—TR.

112. Spirits and angels know that there are inhabitants on the moon too, and equally on the moons or satellites around the planets Jupiter and Saturn. Those who have not seen spirits from there and talked with them are still in no doubt that there are people on these moons, because they are just as much worlds; and where there is a world, man is to be found. Man is the purpose for which a world exists, and the supreme Creator made nothing without a purpose. Anyone whose reason is at all enlightened can be sure that the purpose of creation is the human race, so that heaven can be formed from it.

The Reasons Why the Lord Chose to Be Born in Our World and Not in Another

113. There are many reasons, as I was informed from heaven, why the Lord was pleased to be born and take on human nature in our world and not in another. *The chief cause was for the sake of the Word, which could thus be written in our world; and having been written, could be circulated throughout the world; and once circulated, could be preserved for all posterity, thus enabling it to be made plain that God became man, even to all in the next life.*

114. *The chief cause was for the sake of the Word.* This is because the Word is Divine truth itself, which teaches us that there is a God, a heaven and a hell, and life after death; it also teaches us how to live and what to believe, to enable us to reach heaven and so to be happy for ever. All of these points would be totally unknown without a revelation, which in this world means without the Word. Yet man was created in such a way that he could not die, as far as his interiors are concerned.[36]

115. *The Word could be written in our world,* because the art of writing existed here from the most ancient times, at first on tablets, then on parchment, later on paper, and finally it could be disseminated in print. The Lord's providence caused this for the sake of the Word.

116. *The Word could then be circulated throughout this world,* because all peoples here are in contact, not only by travels abroad, but also by voyages to every part of the globe. Thus the Word, once written, could be spread from one people to another and be taught everywhere.

117. *The Word, once written, could be preserved for all posterity,* that is, for thousands and thousands of years. As is well known, it has been so preserved.

118. *This enabled it to be made plain that God became man.* This is the first and most essential purpose of the Word's existence. For no one can believe in God and love Him, unless he can grasp Him in some form. Consequently those who acknowledge an invisible and therefore incomprehensible deity slip into thinking of nature as god, and so come to believe in no god at all. The Lord was therefore pleased to be born here, and to make that known by means of the Word, so that it should be known, not only on this globe, but *by this means it should be made plain to spirits and angels from other worlds too, as well as to the heathen from our world.*[37]

119. It needs to be known that the Word in our world, which was given to us by the Lord by means of heaven, is the bond which unites heaven and the world. It is for this purpose that everything in the literal sense of the Word corresponds to Divine things in heaven, and the Word in its highest and innermost sense refers to the Lord, His kingdom in the heavens and on earth, love and faith coming from Him and directed to Him, and so life coming from and being in Him. These subjects are what is presented to the angels in heaven, when the Word of our world is read and preached.[38]

120. In every other world Divine truth is made known by word of mouth by means of spirits and angels, as I said earlier when reporting on the inhabitants of the worlds of this solar system. But this is restricted to family groups, for in most worlds the human race lives apart divided into families. Divine truth so revealed by means of spirits and angels does not therefore spread far beyond family groups, and unless renewed by a succession of revelations it is perverted or lost. In our world it is different, for here Divine truth, which is the Word, remains intact in perpetuity.

121. It needs to be known that the Lord acknowledges and accepts all from whatever world they come, who acknowledge and worship God in human form, since the Lord is God in human form. Since the Lord appears to the inhabitants of these worlds in the form of an angel, which means in human form, when the spirits and angels from these worlds are told by the spirits and angels from our world that God is truly Man, they accept that saying, recognising and pleased that it is so.

122. In addition to the reasons already noted, the inhabitants and spirits of our world answer in the Grand Man to the natural and external sense. This sense is the ultimate point at which the interiors of life come to an end, and in which they come to rest as on their common base. Divine truth in the letter, which we call the Word, is similar; and it was for this reason that it was given in this world and not in another.[39] And because the Lord is the Word, and its First and Last, it was so that everything should come into being in proper order that He chose to be born in this world, and to become the Word. This is in agreement with John's words:

> In the beginning there was the Word, and the Word was with God and the Word was God. This was in the beginning with God. All things were made by His means, and nothing that was made was made without Him. *And the Word was made flesh, and lived among us, and we saw His glory, the glory as of the only son of the Father.* No one has ever seen God, but the only son, who is in the Father's bosom, He has explained Him. (John 1:1–4, 14, 18)

The Word is the Lord in respect of Divine truth, and so Divine truth coming from the Lord.[40] But this is a mystery which few can understand.

The Worlds in the Starry Sky

123. Those in heaven are able to speak and associate with angels and spirits coming not only from the worlds of this solar system, but also from worlds in space beyond the solar system. This is true not only of their spirits and angels, but also of their actual inhabitants; but only with those whose interiors are open, so that they can hear those speaking from heaven. A person can do the same while living in the world, if the Lord permits him to speak with spirits and angels. For man is, in respect of his interiors, a spirit. The body he carries round with him in the world is only to enable him to function in this ultimate sphere, the natural or earthly one.

But no one is allowed to talk with spirits and angels as if he were a spirit himself, unless he is, as regards faith and love, capable of associating with angels. Nor is this association possible, unless his faith and love are directed to the

Lord. For it is by means of faith and love to Him, that is, by the truths of teaching and a life of good actions coming from Him, that man is linked to Him. When he is so linked, he is safe from the assaults of wicked spirits from hell. Others cannot have their interiors opened to such an extent, since they are not in the Lord. This is why there are few today allowed to talk and converse with angels. An obvious proof of this is the fact that to-day there is hardly any belief in the existence of spirits and angels, let alone their presence with every person, and that these put a person in touch with heaven, and through heaven with the Lord. Even less do people believe that when a person's body dies, his spirit lives on and in human form as before death.

124. Since many in the church today lack any belief in life after death, and almost all belief in heaven and in the Lord as the God of heaven and earth, I have had the interiors of my spirit opened by the Lord, so that I can, while remaining in the body, be together with angels in heaven, not only talking with them, but seeing the astonishing sights of heaven and describing them. This may prevent them afterwards asking, who has come from heaven to us and reported on its existence and what it contains? But I know that those who have previously denied in their hearts the existence of heaven and hell, and life after death, will become all the more set in their unbelief and continue to deny their existence. It is easier to turn a raven white than to turn those who have once rejected belief at heart into believers. This is because they always take a negative, never a positive, view of such matters. So let what I have so far said and shall say further about spirits and angels be addressed to the few who do believe. However, to guide the

rest to some sort of acknowledgment, I have been allowed
to report facts likely to entertain and excite the attention of
the curious; so I shall also report now on the worlds in the
starry sky.

125. Anyone ignorant of the mysteries of heaven finds it
impossible to believe that anyone can see worlds so remote, and report anything about them learned by the experience of the senses. But he should know that the spaces
and distances, and therefore movements, to be found in
the natural world are in their origin and first cause changes
of state in interiors, and it is these which determine the appearance of space and distance for angels and spirits.[41]
Passing from one state to another gives them the appearance of passing from one place to another, and from one
world to another, even to worlds on the edge of the universe. The same thing can happen to a person's spirit,
while his body still remains fixed in its position. This is
what happened to me, since by the Lord's Divine mercy I
was allowed to associate with spirits as a spirit and at the
same time with men as a man. Anyone who relies on his
senses cannot understand how a person can travel in spirit,
since he is restricted to time and space and measures his
movements in those terms.

126. Anyone can establish for himself the existence of
many worlds from the large number of stars to be seen in
space. It is well known in the learned world that each star
is in its own region like a sun, keeping its fixed position as
the sun of our world does its; it is its distance which makes
it appear as small as a star. It follows that like our sun it has
planets round it, which are worlds. These are invisible to
our eyes because of their immense distance, and because
they shine only with light reflected from their own star,

which again cannot reach us here. What other purpose can such a vast sky with so many constellations serve? Man is the purpose for which the universe was created, so that he should people heaven with angels. And in the eyes of an infinite Creator, how insignificant would the human race be, and the heaven composed of angels from one world, seeing that a thousand, or even tens of thousands of worlds would not be enough for Him.

(2) It has been calculated that if there were a million worlds in the universe, and three hundred million human beings in each world, and two hundred generations in six thousand years, and if each human being or spirit were given a space of three cubic metres*, the total number of people or spirits, if all added together, would still not occupy a thousandth part of the volume of this world, but perhaps the volume of one of the satellites of the planets Jupiter or Saturn. Such a volume would be beneath notice on the scale of the universe, since these satellites are barely visible to the naked eye. How insignificant would this be to the Creator of the universe, who, being infinite, would not be satisfied even if they filled the whole universe?

(3) I talked with angels on this subject, and they said that they shared a similar idea about the small size of the human race compared with the infinite size of the Creator; but their thinking was in terms of states, not space. In their opinion as many myriads of worlds as could ever be imagined would still be as nothing to the Lord. However, I shall in what follows report on the worlds in the starry sky from direct experience. This will show how my spirit was able to travel to such places, while my body remained in its own place.

---

*An approximation; the original uses a word meaning *ell*. —TR.

The First World in the Starry Sky, and Its Spirits and Inhabitants: A Report Based on Things Heard and Seen

127. Under the Lord's guidance I was taken by angels to a world in the starry sky, where I was allowed to look at the world itself, but not to talk with its inhabitants, only with spirits from it. All the inhabitants or people of each world become spirits when their life in the world is over, and they remain in the vicinity of their own world. I was, however, able to gather information from them about their world and the condition of its inhabitants. For when people leave the body, they take with them their whole previous life and everything in their memory.[42]

(2) Being taken to worlds in space does not mean being taken or travelling in body, but in spirit. The spirit is guided through varying states of inner life, which appear to him like travels through space.[41] Agreement or similarity in states of life determines how close people come, for agreement or similarity of life links them, disagreement or dissimilarity separates them. This can allow it to be seen how travel in spirit takes place, and how one can approach distant places, while the person still keeps to his same place.

(3) But taking spirits by changes of inner state outside their own globe, making the changes advance by stages until a state is reached which agrees with or resembles that of the people to whom they are being taken, is something only the Lord can do. For there must be continuous guidance and planned advance from first to last, on both outward and return journeys. It especially needs the Lord's help for this to happen to a person who in body is still in the world of nature, and consequently subject to spatial constraints. Those who are dependent on the impressions conveyed by the bodily senses, and think only in these terms, cannot be brought to believe this actually happened.

(4) The reason is that the bodily senses cannot grasp the idea of travel without movement through space. But those whose thinking comes from the senses of the spirit a little withdrawn or distanced from the body's senses can be brought to believe and grasp it, since inner thinking has no concept of space or time, but their place is taken by the things which give rise to space and time. It is therefore for these people that the following reports on the worlds in the starry sky are intended, not for the others, unless they are the sort of people who will allow themselves to be instructed.

128. While fully awake I was taken by angels under the Lord's guidance to one of the worlds in space, accompanied by some spirits from this globe. We travelled towards the right for a period of two hours. Around the limits of our solar system there was first to be seen a shining, but dense, cloud. After it came fiery smoke coming up from a great gap. It was a huge chasm, which in that direction separates our solar system from that of some stars. The fiery smoke could be seen at quite a long distance. I was taken through the middle of it, and then below me in that gap or chasm were to be seen large numbers of people, who were spirits. (Spirits are all to be seen in human form, and really are people.) I also heard them talking to one another, but I was not able to learn where they came from or what they were like. However, one of them told me that they were guards, set to prevent spirits passing from this system into another in space, unless given permission.

Confirmation that this was so came from some spirits in my company who, on reaching that great gap, were not allowed to cross; they began to shout out that they were dying. They resembled people struggling in their death-agony. So they stopped this side of that chasm, and could not travel any further. For the fiery smoke rising up from the chasm gripped them and subjected them to these tortures.

129. After travelling through that great gap, I finally reached a place where I could stop. Then some spirits appeared to me overhead, and I was able to talk with them. From their speech and from the way they grasped matters and set them forth, I could clearly observe that they came from another world, for they were quite different from the spirits of our solar system. They too could tell from my speech that I came from a great distance.

130. After talking with them for a while about various matters, I asked what God they worshipped. They replied that it was some angel, who appeared to them as a Divine Man, since he shone with light. They said that he teaches them and allows them to perceive what they ought to do. They went on to say that they knew that the greatest God was in the sun of the heaven of angels; He appeared to their angel, but not to themselves. He was too mighty for them to dare to worship Him. The angel whom they worshipped was a community of angels, which the Lord had appointed to oversee them, teaching them the way of justice and right. They therefore had light from a kind of flame, looking like a small torch, rather fiery and yellow. The reason for this is that they do not venerate the Lord, so they cannot get light from the sun of the heaven of angels, but only from a community of angels. Such a community can, when permitted by the Lord, provide light to spirits of a lower region. I too saw that community of angels; it was high above them, and I also saw the flame which shed the light.

131. In other respects they were restrained, rather simple, but still right-thinking enough. The light they had allowed one to infer the nature of their intellectual faculty. For understanding depends upon the way the light of heaven is received, since it is Divine truth proceeding from the Lord as sun which gives light and allows angels not only to see but also to understand.[43]

132. I was informed that the inhabitants and spirits of that world answer in the Grand Man to something in the

SPLEEN. Confirmation of this came from an influence I felt on the spleen while they were talking with me.

133. I asked them about the sun of their system which gives light to their world. They said that the sun there looks flame-coloured. When I pictured to them the size of the sun of our world, they declared that theirs was smaller; for their sun is to our eyes a star. I heard from angels that it is one of the smaller stars. They also said that the starry sky was visible from their world too, and a star larger than the rest is to be seen to the west of them. I was told from heaven that this is our sun.

134. After a while my sight was opened so that I could to some extent look at the world itself. There were many meadows to be seen, and woods with leafy trees, as well as sheep with woolly fleeces. Later I saw a few of the inhabitants; they were of the lower classes, dressed in very much the same kind of costume as peasants in Europe. I also saw a gentleman with his lady; she had a fine figure and behaved becomingly. So did the man; but I was surprised to see he had a lordly, almost haughty, walk. The lady, however, walked humbly. The angels told me that this is the custom in that world, and that such men are loved because they are none the less good. I was further told that they are not allowed to have more than one wife, because this is against their laws.

The lady whom I saw had a broad garment covering her chest, behind which she could hide. It was made so that one could put one's arms into it and so put it on, and thus be lost to view. Its lower part could be tucked up; when tucked up and held close to the body it looked like the bodices worn by women in our world. But the same garment could also be worn by a man. A gentleman was

seen to take one from a lady and put it round his back, and
when he unfastened the lower part it fell to his feet like a
gown, and he walked off wearing it like this. What I saw in
that world, I saw not with my bodily eyes, but with the
eyes of my spirit. A spirit is able to see things in a world,
when permitted to do so by the Lord.

135. Since I am aware that people will doubt the possibility of a person ever being able to see with the eyes of his
spirit anything in a world so remote, I should like to explain how this can happen. Distance in the next life is unlike distance in this world, because in the next life it
depends entirely on a person's inward state. Those who
share a like state are together in one community and in one
place. Presence there is always the result of likeness of
state, distance the result of unlikeness of state. This is how
it was that I was in the vicinity of that world, when the
Lord brought me into a state resembling that of its spirits
and inhabitants, so that I could then be present and talk
with them. This shows plainly that in the spiritual world inhabited planets are not spatially remote as in the natural
world, but only appear to be so, depending on the state of
life of their spirits and inhabitants. By state of life I mean
the state of their affections as regards love and faith. I
should also like to explain how it is that a spirit, or what is
the same, a person in his spirit, can see things on a planet.

(2) Neither spirits nor angels can see anything in the
world by using their own sight; for to them the world's
light, that is, sunlight, is like thick darkness. In the same
way neither can a person with his bodily sight see anything
in the next life, for to him the light of heaven is like thick
darkness. But still spirits and angels can, at the Lord's
good pleasure, see things in the world through a person's

eyes. The Lord, however, only permits this in the case of those whom He allows to talk with spirits and angels and be present with them. They were allowed to see things in this world, and as clearly as I do, by using my eyes. They could also hear people talking with me. It has sometimes happened that spirits have through me seen friends, whom they had known while living in the body, as vividly present as previously, and have been astonished. They have even seen their husbands and children, and wanted to tell them they were there and could see them, asking me to tell them how they were in the next life. But I was forbidden to tell them this and to disclose that they had been seen, especially because they would have called me mad, or at least thought these were mental delusions, as I was well aware that despite their verbal professions they did not at heart believe in the existence of spirits, that the dead have risen again, and are present among spirits; nor in the possibility of their seeing and hearing by means of a person.

(3) When my inner sight was first opened and those in the next life saw the world and things in it through my eyes, they were so astonished that they called it the greatest of miracles, and felt a new joy at the possibility of earth communicating with heaven and heaven with earth. Although this joy lasted for months, it has now become so familiar to them that they are no longer surprised at it. I was informed that the spirits and angels with other people do not see anything at all in the world, but only perceive the thoughts and affections of those with whom they are.

(4) From these facts it can be established that man was so created that, while living among people in the world, he would at the same time live in heaven among angels, and conversely. He was likewise so created that heaven and the world could be simultaneously present with him and act

together, and so that people should know what happens in heaven, and angels should know what happens in the world. When people die, they are thus able to pass from the Lord's kingdom on earth to His kingdom in the heavens, not as if entering a new one, but the same one that they lived in while in the body. But by becoming immersed in bodily matters man has shut himself off from heaven.

136. To end with I talked with the spirits from that world about various achievements of our world. I told them especially about our possession of sciences unknown elsewhere, such as astronomy, geometry, mechanics, physics, chemistry, medicine, optics and philosophy. I went on to mention techniques unknown elsewhere, such as ship-building, the casting of metals, writing on paper, the diffusion of writings by printing, thus allowing communication with other people in the world, and the preservation for posterity of written material for thousands of years. I told them that this had happened with the Word given by the Lord, so that there was a revelation permanently operating in our world.

137. Finally I was shown the hell occupied by those from that world. The sight of those from it was extremely terrifying. I could not dare to describe their monstrous faces. I also saw there sorceresses who practise dreadful tricks. These were seen dressed in green, and they struck horror into me.

The Second World in the Starry Sky, and Its Spirits and Inhabitants

138. Afterwards I was brought by the Lord to a world in space, which was even further away from our world than the first one I have described. It became plain that it was more distant, because the journey to it in my spirit lasted two days. This world lay to the left, the previous one to the right. Remoteness in the spiritual world does not depend on spatial distance, but on difference of state, as was said above. I was therefore able to deduce from the time the journey to it took, two whole days, that the state of the interiors affecting people there, that is, the state of their affections and consequently of their thoughts, is so very different from those affecting spirits from our world. Since I was transported there by changes of interior state, I was able to observe the successive changes as they happened up to my arrival. This took place while I was awake.

139. On my arrival there I did not see the world, but I saw spirits from it. For, as I said before, the spirits of each world are to be seen around their own world, because their characters resemble those of the people who live there. They have come from them, and are there to be of service to them. These spirits were seen very high overhead, and from that position they could watch my arrival. It should be known that in the next life those who stand on high can watch those below them; and the higher they are the wider their field of vision. They can not only watch them, but also talk with them.

They noticed from their position that I was not from their world, but from some distant place. So they spoke to me from there, asking about various matters; and I was able to reply to their questions. Amongst other things I told them which world I was from and what it was like. Afterwards I told them about the planets in our solar system. I also told them about the spirits of the world or planet of Mercury, and how they travel to many worlds in order to acquire knowledge of various matters. On hearing this they said that they too had seen them on a visit.

140. I was told by angels from our world that the inhabitants and spirits from that world answer in the Grand Man to ACUITY OF VISION, and that is why they are to be seen high up; they actually have exceedingly sharp sight. Since this was what they answered to, and they could see acutely what was below them, in course of conversation I actually compared them to eagles, flying high and keeping a sharp watch all round far and wide. But this made them indignant, as they thought I believed them to be like eagles in seeking prey, and thus to be wicked. But I replied that it was not as hunters but for their sharp sight that I had likened them to eagles.

141. When questioned about the God they worshipped, they replied that they worship a God who is visible and invisible; a God visible in human form and invisible without any form. I learned from what they said as well as from the ideas they were thinking about, which were shared with me, that their visible God was in fact our Lord; and they also called Him the Lord. To this I was able to reply that in our world too God is worshipped as invisible and visible, the invisible God being called the Father, and the visible God the Lord. But the two of them are one, as He taught us when He said that they had never seen the appearance of the Father, but the Father and He were one; anyone seeing Him saw the Father, and the Father was in Him and He was in the Father. Consequently both those Divinities were in one Person. These are the Lord's words; see John 5:37; 10:30; 14:7, 9–11.

142. A little later I saw some of the other spirits from the same world, who were to be seen at a lower level than those with whom I had been talking. These, however, were idolaters, worshipping an idol of stone, resembling a human being, but not a beautiful one. It should be known that on arrival in the next life all begin by practising worship like that they had in the world, but they are by stages withdrawn from it. The reason for this is that all worship remains implanted in a person's inner life, and it can only be withdrawn and uprooted by stages.

On seeing this I was able to tell them that they ought not to worship what is dead, but what is alive. They replied to this, saying that they knew that God is alive and is not a stone, but that when they view a stone which resembles a human being they think of a living God. They found it impossible any otherwise to concentrate the ideas of their thought and direct them to an invisible God. Then I was able to tell them that the ideas of thought can be concentrated and directed towards an invisible God, when they are directed towards the Lord, who can be thought of as God visible in human form. By this means man can be linked to an invisible God by thought and affection, and so by faith and love, when he is linked to the Lord, but not in any other way.

143. The spirits who were seen at a height were asked whether in their world people lived under the rule of princes or kings. Their reply to this was that they did not know what kingdoms were, but that they lived under their own government, divided into clans, families and households. Asked whether they were safe living like that, they said they were, since one family never envied another or wanted to take anything from them. They were annoyed at such questions, as if they were being accused of having enemies or taking precautions against robbers. What more does anyone need, they asked, than to have food and clothing, and so to live contented and in peace under one's own government?

144. Asked further about their world they said it contained meadows, flower-gardens and woods full of fruit-bearing trees, as well as lakes with fish in them. There are blue-coloured birds with golden feathers, and animals both large and small. Among the smaller ones they mentioned some which have a raised back like camels in our world. However, they did not eat their flesh, but only that of fish, together with fruit from the trees and vegetables from the earth. They went on to say that they did not build houses to live in, but lived in woodland, where they made roofs among the leaves to shelter from rain and the heat of the sun.

145. When asked about their sun, which is a star visible from our world, they said it has a fiery aspect, appearing no larger than a man's head. I was told by angels that the star which is their sun is one of the smaller ones, not far from the celestial equator.

146. I saw spirits who looked as they had done when they were living in their world. Their faces were not unlike those of people in our world, except that their eyes were small, and so were their noses. This seemed to me rather ugly, but they said that small eyes and noses are a mark of beauty to them.

I saw a woman wearing a gown patterned with roses of different colours. So I asked where in that world they got their clothes. They replied that they gather from plants material which they spin into thread, and they arrange the threads in layers* of double or triple thickness, wetting the cloth with a sticky liquid to give it consistency, and subsequently colouring the woven cloth with herbal dyes. I was given a demonstration of how they make thread. The women sit half-lying† on the ground and use their toes to twist it, and when twisted they pull it towards themselves and work it up with their hands.

---

*Reading *stratim* for *statim* from *Arcana Coelestia* §10163.—Tr.
†Reading *demisupinatae* from *Arcana Coelestia* §10164.—Tr.

147. They also told me that in their world a husband has only one wife, never more. They have as many as ten to fifteen children. There are, they added, also prostitutes to be found there; but these on becoming spirits after their life in the body are sorceresses, who are thrown into hell.

12

The Third World in the Starry Sky, and Its Spirits and Inhabitants

148. Some spirits became visible far off, who were unwilling to come close. The reason was that they could not bear the company of the spirits from our world who were then around me. I realised from this that they came from another world. I was told afterwards that they came from a certain world in space, but I was given no indication where it might be. These spirits utterly refused to think about their bodies, or indeed about anything to do with the body or matter; in this they were quite different from the spirits of our world. This was why they were unwilling to come close; but when some of the spirits from our world had been sent away, they came closer and talked with me.

However, I then had a feeling of unease, which is

caused by the clash of spheres. All spirits and communities of spirits are surrounded by spiritual spheres.[26] These proceed from the life of their affections and so their thoughts, so when their affections are opposed, there is a clash leading to uneasiness. The spirits from our world reported that neither did they dare to get close to them, because when they did, they not only felt gripped by uneasiness, but even seemed to themselves to be tied hand and foot with snakes, which they could not untie until the spirits left. This appearance is due to the correspondence. The spirits of our world answer in the Grand Man to the external senses or bodily sense-perception, and in the other life this is pictured by snakes.[44]

149. Since this is the nature of the spirits of that world, they do not look to the eyes of other spirits to have a clearly human form, as others do; but they resemble clouds, in most cases a dark cloud, with some human whiteness mixed in it. But they said that they were white inside, and on becoming angels this dark appearance is turned to a lovely blue. This too was displayed to me. I asked them whether they had had such an idea of their bodies when they were living in their world. They said that the people of their world thought nothing of their bodies, but only of the spirit it contained, knowing that this would live for ever, but the body would perish. They also reported that many in their world believe the spirit in the body to have existed from eternity and to have been introduced into the body at conception. But they went on to say that they now know this to be untrue, and they were sorry to have held such a false belief.

150. When I asked whether they would like to see some scenes in our world, something which they could do

through my eyes (see §135 above), they replied first that
they could not, and then that they did not want to, since
they would see nothing but earthly and material objects,
things they banished from their thoughts to the best of
their ability. Still some magnificent palaces were pictured
for them, resembling those where kings and princes live in
our world. Such scenes can be depicted to spirits so vividly
that it seems as if they were really there. However, the spirits from that world thought nothing of them, calling them
marble images; and then they reported that they have
more magnificent ones, and these are their sacred temples,
built not of stone but of wood. When they were told that
these were still earthly, they replied that they were not, but
heavenly, since when they look at them it is not earthly but
heavenly ideas which fill their minds, and they believe that
they will also see similar sights in heaven after death.

151. They then depicted their sacred temples before the
spirits of our world, who said that they had never seen anything more magnificent. I can describe them, because I too
saw them. They are built not of felled trees, but of ones
growing in their native soil. They said that their world contained trees of wonderful height and size. From their earliest
stages they arrange these trees in rows to form porticoes and
walkways, shaping the branches while still supple, and cut-
ting and pruning them, so that as they grow they will inter-
lace and join to make the floor and pavement of the temple.
They make the branches at the sides grow up to form walls,
and overhead bend them into arches to make a roof. From
these materials they construct with admirable skill a temple
raised high above the ground. They make a way up composed of branches stretched out horizontally with no space
between and firmly bound together. In addition they deco-

rate such a temple both inside and out with various kinds of topiary work; and so they build up whole parks.

But I was not allowed to see what these temples were like inside. I was only told that sunlight is admitted through openings between the branches, and is everywhere passed through crystals, which turn the light around the walls into colours like the rainbow, especially shades of blue and orange, which they particularly like. This is their architecture, which they prefer to the most magnificent palaces of our world.

152. They went on to say that the inhabitants of that world do not live high up, but at ground level in low huts. This is because heights are for the Lord who is in heaven, low dwellings for people on earth. I was also shown their huts. They were rectangular, having inside a bed running without a break round the walls, in which they sleep one next to another. On the side opposite the entrance there is a round recess with a table in front, and a hearth behind. This provides light for the whole room. They do not have a fire burning on the hearth, but some glowing wood which emits as much light as the flame of a fire. They said that towards evening time these logs look as if they had embers of fire in them.

153. They said that they do not live in communities, but in separate households. They form communities when they meet for worship; then those who teach walk below the temple, the rest in the porticoes at the side. These meetings afford them inward joys from looking at the temple and the worship conducted in it.

154. On the subject of Divine worship they said that they acknowledged God in human form, that is, our Lord. For any who acknowledge the God of the universe in human form are acceptable to the Lord and are guided by Him. The rest cannot be guided, since their thought is shapeless. They added that the inhabitants of their world are taught about things in heaven by some kind of direct contact with angels and spirits. It is easier for them than for others to be brought into contact by the Lord, because they banish bodily things from their thoughts and affections.

I asked what happens to wicked people among them. They said no one was allowed in their world to behave badly, but if anyone had wicked thoughts and did wicked deeds, he is rebuked by a certain spirit, who threatens him with death if he persists in wrongdoing. If he still persists, he loses consciousness and dies. In this way the people of that world are saved from being infected by the wicked.

One of the spirits of this kind was sent to me, to talk with me as he does with the wicked. In addition he caused me a certain amount of pain in the abdominal region, saying that this was what he did to those who have wicked thoughts and do wicked deeds, threatening them with death if they persisted. They said that those who profane sacred things are severely punished. Before the spirit appears to punish them, they have a vision of a lion's jaws gaping wide open, livid in colour, looking as if it intended to swallow their head and tear it from the body. This gives them a dreadful fright. They call the spirit who punishes them a devil.

155. Since they wanted to know how revelation took place in our world, I told them that it was by means of writing and preaching based on the Word, not by direct contact with spirits and angels. I told them that writings could be printed, so that whole groups of people could read and understand them, and so have their way of life improved. They were very surprised to hear of the existence of such a technique, which is wholly unknown elsewhere. But they grasped that in this world, where bodily and earthly matters are so popular, there was no other way divine influences from heaven could be felt and received. It would be dangerous for such people to talk with angels.

156. The spirits of that world are to be seen up above on a level with the head, towards the right. All spirits can be told apart by their position relative to the human body. This happens because the whole of heaven corresponds in every part to a human being.[6] The spirits remain at this level and distance, because their correspondence is not with a person's exteriors, but his interiors. They act upon the left knee, a little above and below the joint, imparting a kind of very noticeable vibration. This is a sign that they correspond to *the linking of natural and celestial elements*.

The Fourth World in the Starry Sky, and Its Spirits and Inhabitants

157. I was taken to yet another world in space outside the solar system; this was brought about by changes in my mental state, changes, that is, affecting my spirit. For, as I have said several times before, a spirit is taken from place to place by nothing but changes in his inner state. These changes seem to him exactly like movement from one place to another or travelling. It took around ten hours of continuous changes for me to reach their state of life from my own, so for me to travel there in my spirit. I was travelling eastwards, towards the left, and I seemed to be gradually climbing above the horizontal plane. I was also able to watch clearly my progress and advance from my previous position, until at length those I had left behind disappeared from view. Meanwhile I conversed on various subjects with the spirits accompanying me.

We had with us a certain spirit who during his life in the world had been a most impassioned prelate and preacher as well as writer. My spirit companions thought from my idea of him that he must be an outstanding Christian at heart. For in the world an idea is formed and a judgment made based on a person's preaching and writings, rather than on his life, if this is not manifest; and if there seems to be anything discordant in his life, excuses are offered. For the idea formed, one's thought and perception about anyone, puts a favourable gloss on everything about him.

158. When I noticed that I had in spirit travelled in the starry sky far outside the solar system (as was evident from the changes of state and what seemed like continuous movement lasting almost ten hours), I at length heard spirits talking in the vicinity of some world, which later on became visible to me. When I approached them, they said after some conversation that they sometimes have visitors from elsewhere, who talk with them about God and confuse their thinking. They also pointed out the route by which they come, which allowed me to realise that they were spirits from our world. When I asked in what way they confused them, they said it was by declaring that one ought to believe in a Divinity divided into three Persons, although they still called them one God. When they investigated the way these visitors thought, their concept was revealed as a Trinity, not continuous, but separate. Some regarded the Trinity as three Persons conversing with one another; others as two Persons sitting next to each other, and the third listening to them and going out from them. Yet they called each Person God, and although they have a different concept of each, they still speak of a single God. They complained bitterly that the visitors confused them by thinking of three but saying one, when in fact one ought to think as one speaks and speak as one thinks.

(2) The spirit with me, who had been a prelate and preacher in the world, was also then investigated, to see what his concept was of one God and three Persons; he pictured three Gods, but joined together to form one. But this threefold unity was represented as invisible, because it was Divine. When this idea was presented, it was perceived that he was only thinking about the Father and not about the Lord, and that his concept of an invisible God was nothing but a concept of nature in its first beginnings. As a result, the inmost level of nature was his Divinity, so that he could easily be brought to acknowledge nature as God. It needs to be known that in the next life anyone's concept of anything is pictured vividly, so that investigation is possible into each person's thought and perception on matters of faith. The concept of God is the principal one in everyone's thinking; for if it is a true one, it is the means which links him with the Divine and consequently with heaven.

(3) Then when these spirits were asked what was their concept of God, they replied that it was not of an invisible God, but God visible in human form. They knew this not only by perceiving it inwardly, but also from the fact that He had appeared to them as a man. They added that if they thought of God as invisible, as some of their visitors did, that is to say, devoid of form and quality, they found it totally impossible to think about God, since anything invisible like this cannot be reduced to a concept one can think about.

On hearing this I was allowed to tell them that they were right to think of God in human form, and that many people from our world have a similar idea, especially when thinking about the Lord. I told them that the ancients too thought like this, and related the stories of Abraham, Lot, Gideon and Manoah and his wife, as they are set forth in our Word. All these saw God in human form, and acknowledged Him whom they saw as the Creator of the universe, calling Him Jehovah; this too came from inward perception. But this inward perception has now been lost in the Christian world, and remains only with simple folk who have faith.

159. Before being told this, they thought that our company too belonged to those who wanted to confuse them about God by conceiving Him as three. So they were pleased to hear this, and said that messengers have been sent to them too by God, whom they then called the Lord, to teach them about Himself. They said they did not want to admit visitors who upset them, especially by speaking of three Persons in the Divinity, since they know that God is one and consequently there is one Divine, not a unanimous group of three. But perhaps they were willing to think of God as being like an angel, in whom the inmost level of life is the invisible element which allows him to think and be wise, the outward level of life is the element visible in human form which allows him to see and act, and the outgoing life is the sphere of love and faith radiating from him, for each spirit or angel has a sphere of life, which allows him to be recognised at a distance.[26] As regards the Lord, the life going forth from Him is the Divinity Itself, which fills the heavens and makes them to be heavens, because it goes forth from the very Being of a life of love and faith. They said that this was the only way they could perceive the Trinity and the Unity [of God] at once.

(2) On hearing this I was allowed to say that such a concept of a Trinity co-existing with a Unity is in agreement with the concept angels have of the Lord. For He teaches that the Father and He are one, and that the Father is in Him and He is in the Father; that he who sees Him sees the Father, and he who believes in Him believes in and knows the Father. He also teaches that the Comforter, whom He calls the Spirit of truth, as well as the Holy Spirit, goes forth from Him, and does not speak of His own accord, but what the Lord says; by this is meant the Divine which goes forth.

(3) I went on to suggest that the concept of a Trinity co-existing with a Unity is in agreement with the Being and the Coming-into-being of the Lord's life, when He was in the world. The Being of His life was the Divine Itself, since He was conceived of Jehovah. The being of anyone's life is the source from which he was conceived. The Coming-into-being of the life from that Being is the human in form. The being of everyone's life which he has from his father is called the soul, and the coming-into-being of life from that source is called the body. Soul and body make up a single person. The analogy between them is as between what is contained in effort and what is in the resultant action, for an act is an effort in action, so that the two are one. Effort in a person is called the will, and effort in action is called an act. The body is the instrument by means of which the principal, that is, the will, acts; and instrument and principal are one in acting. So it is with the soul and body, and this is the concept of them held by angels in heaven. From this they know that the Lord made His Human Divine by the Divine in Himself, which was His soul derived from the Father.

Moreover, the creed everywhere accepted in the Christian world is not against this, for it teaches:

> Although Christ is God and Man, yet He is not two, but one Christ. Indeed, He is wholly one and a single person; because, as the body and the soul are one man, so too God and Man is one Christ.[45]

Because there was such a union, or such a unity, in the Lord, He rose again not only as to the soul, but also as to the body, which He glorified in the world, unlike any man. He also taught His disciples about this, saying:

> Feel me and see, for a spirit does not have flesh and bones, as you see me have.[46] [Luke 24:39.]

The spirits could perfectly well understand these words, since they fall within the grasp of angelic spirits. They then added that the Lord alone has power in the heavens, and the heavens are His. In reply to this I was able to tell them that the church in our world also knows this from the Lord's words spoken before He went up into heaven. For He then said:

> All power has been given me in heaven and on earth. [Matt. 28:18.]

160. Afterwards I talked with those spirits about their world. All spirits have this knowledge, when their natural or outer memory is laid open by the Lord; for they bring this with them from the world, but it is only laid open at the Lord's good pleasure. Then the spirits reported about the world they came from, saying that when they receive permission they appear to the inhabitants of their world, and talk with them as if they were living people. This comes about by their being allowed into their natural or outer memory, so that they can recall what they thought while living in the world. The inhabitants then have their inner sight, the sight of their spirits, opened, so that the spirits become visible to them. They added that the inhabitants are unaware that they are not people in their world, and it only dawns on them they are not, when the spirits suddenly disappear from view.

I told them that the same thing happened in our world in ancient times, in front, for instance of Abraham, Sarah, Lot, the inhabitants of Sodom, Manoah and his wife, Joshua, Mary, Elizabeth and the Prophets as a class. The Lord also appeared in the same way, and those who saw Him did not know that He was not a man in the world, until He revealed Himself. This, I said, rarely happened at the present time, because people should not be forced to believe by such means. For a forced belief, such as is induced by miracles, does not stick, and could also be damaging to those who might have belief established in them by means of the Word without any coercion.

161. The spirit who in the world had been a prelate and preacher did not at all believe in the existence of worlds other than ours, because he had thought in the world that this was the only world in which the Lord was born, and no one could be saved without the Lord. He was therefore brought into a state similar to that of the spirits when they appear in their own world like people, as mentioned above. In this state he was sent into that world, so that he could not only see it, but also talk with its inhabitants. After this I too was allowed to enter into communication with it, so that I likewise saw the inhabitants and some scenes upon that planet (see §135 above). Four kinds of people were displayed, each kind replacing the other in turn. First I saw people wearing clothes; then some who were naked and the colour of human flesh; then some naked, but with inflamed bodies; and finally some who were black.

162. When the spirit who had been a prelate and preacher was in the company of those who wore clothes, a woman was seen with an extremely pretty face; she was dressed in a simple garment, a tunic which hung down becomingly at the back and was put on over the arms. She wore a beautiful head-covering in the form of a garland of flowers. The spirit was very much delighted at the sight of this young lady, and he started talking to her and taking hold of her hand. But she, realising he was a spirit and not from her world, tore herself away from him.

Afterwards a number of other women were seen by him on his right; they were tending sheep and lambs, which they were then taking to a drinking-trough, fed through a small channel from a lake. They were similarly dressed, holding shepherds' crooks in their hands, with which they brought the sheep and lambs to drink. They said the sheep follow the direction pointed out with their crooks. The sheep seen were large with long, broad and woolly tails. The women's faces seen close up were full and lovely. Men were also seen with faces the colour of human flesh, as in our world. But there was a difference; the lower part of their faces was black instead of bearded, and their noses had a whiter colour than flesh.

(2) Afterwards the spirit, who in the world, as I said before, had been a preacher, was taken further on, but against his will, because he was still thinking about the woman who had so delighted him. This was plain from the fact that a kind of shadow of him was still to be seen where

he had previously been. He then reached the people who were naked. These were to be seen walking about in pairs, being in each case husband and wife. They wore a loin-cloth, and some kind of covering around the head. While in their company the spirit was brought into the state he had been in when he wanted to preach; so he then said that he wanted to preach to them on the Lord crucified. But they said they did not wish to hear such a story, not knowing what it was. They knew, they said, that the Lord is alive. So then he declared that he would preach on the Lord living. But this too they refused to hear, saying that they felt something in his speech that was not heavenly, because there was much in it for his own sake or for the sake of his reputation and honour. They could tell by listening to the sound of his speech whether it came from the heart or not; and being of such a nature he could not teach them. So he fell silent. When living in the world he had been a most eloquent speaker, very skilled in moving his listeners to holy thoughts. But this eloquence had been a skill he learned, so something of his own and from the world, not from heaven.

163. They went on to say that they are able to tell whether those of their people who are naked have the con-jugial principle. They showed how they could tell this from their spiritual concept of marriage, which was communi-cated to me. It was such that a likeness of interiors was formed by the linking of good and truth, that is, of love and faith. The influence of this link flowing down into the body produced conjugial love. For everything on the men-tal level is reproduced by some natural appearance in the body; and this is an appearance of conjugial love, when two people inwardly love each other, and also that love

makes each wish to want and think the same things as the
other, so that they wish the inner levels of their minds to
be together and be joined. As a result the spiritual affection
of their minds becomes a natural affection in the body and
clothes itself with a feeling of conjugial love. The spiritual
affections of their minds is an affection for good and truth
and an impulse to link them; for all mental activities, that
is, activities of thought and will, relate to truth and good.
They also said that no conjugial connexion is possible between one man and several wives, since the marriage of
good and truth, which takes place in people's minds, is impossible except between two partners.

164. Then the spirit mentioned above came to the people
who were naked but had inflamed bodies; and finally to
those who were black, some of them naked, others
clothed. But these two groups lived in different parts of
the same world. For a spirit can be taken in a moment to
distant parts of the world, since he advances and travels not
through space like human beings, but through changes of
state (see §§125, 127 above).[41]

165. Finally I talked with the spirits of that world about
the belief of the inhabitants of our world concerning their
resurrection. I said they were unable to conceive of people
coming into the next life immediately after death, and then
looking like people in face, body, arms and feet, having all
their outward and inward senses. Even less could they believe that they would then wear clothes and have houses
and places to live. This was entirely due to the fact that
most people here base their thinking on bodily sense-impressions, so that they do not believe in the existence of
what they cannot see and touch. Few of them can be withdrawn from outward sense-impressions towards inward

ones, and so be lifted into the light of heaven in which inward impressions can be received. It is for this reason that they cannot have any concept of their soul or spirit as being a person, but think of it as wind, air or some formless breath, which yet contains some vitality. This is the reason that they believe they will only be resurrected at the end of the world, which they call the Last Judgment, thinking that their body, though collapsed into dust and scattered to all the winds, must then be brought back and reunited with their soul or spirit.

(2) I added that they are allowed to hold this belief, because there is no other way that those who, as I said, base their thinking on outward sense-impressions, could think of their soul or spirit living as a person in human form, except by re-entering the body they carried around with them in the world. Unless therefore the body were said to be resurrected, they would at heart reject the teaching on resurrection and everlasting life as incomprehensible.

(3) Yet thinking like this about resurrection has this advantage, that they do believe in a life after death. The consequence of this belief is that, when they lie sick in bed and cease to base their thinking, as previously, on worldly and bodily matters, that is, on sense-impressions, they then believe that they will live again immediately after dying.

At this time they also talk about heaven, and how they hope to live there as soon as they die, putting aside all they have been taught about the Last Judgment. I told them how I have several times been surprised how it is that, when those who have faith talk about life after death and their friends who are dying or have died, without at the same time thinking about the Last Judgment, they believe their friends will live or are living as people immediately after death. The moment they start thinking about the Last Judgment, this idea is changed into a material idea of their earthly body, which has to be reunited with their soul.

(4) For they are unaware that each person is inwardly a spirit, and the life of the body and all its parts comes from the spirit, not from the body by itself. They do not know that it is the spirit which is the real person, sharing its form, but invisible to the body's eyes, being visible only to the eyes of spirits. Hence it is too that, when a person's spirit has its sight opened, which is the result of the withdrawal of the body's sight, angels can be seen as people. So it was that angels appeared to the ancients, as related in the Word.

I have had several conversations with spirits whom I knew when they were people living in the world, and asked whether they wanted to be clothed again with their earthly bodies, as they had previously imagined. On hearing this they ran off to a distance at the mere idea of being reunited, in astonishment at having been led in the world to think so by blind faith without any understanding.

166. In addition I saw in that world their homes, which were low, long houses, with windows in the sides corresponding to the number of apartments or rooms into which they were divided. The roof was rounded, and there was a door at either end. They said that they were built of earth and roofed with turf. The windows were made of grass thread, so woven as to admit light. I also saw some children. They said their neighbours visited them, especially because of their children, so that they could enjoy the company of other children under the eyes and protection of their parents.

There were also fields to be seen which were turning white as the crop was almost ripe. I was shown the seeds or grain of that crop, which resembled the grains of Chinese wheat.* I was also shown loaves made from this, which were small, breaking up into four pieces. Grassy plains with flowers were also to be seen there, as well as trees with fruits like pomegranates. There were shrubs which, though not vines, bore berries from which they prepared wine.

167. The sun there, which is a star to us, looks flame-coloured, about a quarter the size of our sun. Their year is approximately two hundred days, and their day is fifteen hours measured by days in our world. The planet itself is one of the smallest in the starry sky, hardly five hundred German miles† in circumference. These observations were made by angels who had compared the facts about our world, which they had seen through me or in my memory. They reached these conclusions by angelic ideas, which allow them to appreciate instantly the measurements of space and time accurately measured against space and time elsewhere. The ideas of angels, being spiritual, go far beyond those of men, which are natural.

---

*Probably rice. —TR.
†The German mile was equivalent to 6.64 English miles, giving a figure of 3320 miles or about 5300 km for the circumference.—TR.

14

The Fifth World in the Starry Sky, Its Spirits and Inhabitants

168. On another occasion I was taken to yet another world in space outside the solar system. The journey was by means of changes of state lasting for nearly twelve hours without a break. I was accompanied by a number of spirits and angels from our world, with whom I conversed as we progressed on our journey. I travelled at one time obliquely upwards, at another obliquely downwards, but constantly towards the right, which in the next life is towards the south. In only two places did I see any spirits, and in one I spoke with them. This progress or journey allowed me to observe how immense is the Lord's heaven for angels and spirits. The uninhabited regions allowed me to deduce that it is so immense that, if there were many tens of thousands of worlds, each containing as large a population of human beings as ours, there would still be room enough for them to live for ever without filling it up. I reached this conclusion by comparing it with the extent of the heaven surrounding our world and designed for it, which was so small in comparison that it would not equal one hundred millionth part of the uninhabited space.

169. When the angelic spirits from that world came into view, they hailed us asking who we were and what we wanted. We said we were travellers who had been brought to their abode, and they had nothing to fear from us. For they were afraid that we were some of those who disturb their ideas of God, faith and suchlike; it was to avoid them they had retreated in that direction towards their world, seeking somewhere they could escape them. Asked what ideas these visitors used to disturb them, they replied the idea of three [Persons], and of a Divinity in God with no human feature, when all the time they know and perceive that God is one and is a man. Then we grasped that those who upset them and whom they avoided, were from our world. This was also evident from the fact that it is those from our world who in the next life travel around as the result of the fondness and pleasure they take in travel, which they acquired in the world. For in other worlds people do not travel like this. Later we learned that they were monks, who had travelled our globe with the purpose of converting the heathen. We therefore told them that they were right to avoid them, since their motive is not teaching, but gaining advantage and taking control. At first, we said, they aim to ensnare people's minds by various means, but they end up by making them into slaves under their orders. Moreover, we said, they were right not to let such people upset their concept of God.

(2) They went on to say that their visitors also confused them by saying that the spirits of that world ought to have faith and believe what their visitors said. Their reply to this was that they did not know the meaning of faith or believing, since they could perceive in themselves that a thing was so. They came from the Lord's celestial kingdom, where interior perception allows everyone to know truths which we call matters of faith. They are enlightened by the Lord, and in this differ from those in the spiritual kingdom. A further sign that the angelic spirits of that world came from the celestial kingdom was the sight of a flame, which is the source of their ideas. For the light in the celestial kingdom is like a flame, but in the spiritual kingdom brilliant white.

Those from the celestial kingdom when speaking about truths never say more than "yes, yes" or "no, no"; they never reason about whether a matter is so or not. It is these of whom the Lord says:

> Your speech is to be 'yes, yes, no, no'. Anything further is from evil. [Matt. 5:37.]

This is why those spirits said they did not know what it was to have faith or believe. They regard this as being as if someone told his companion, who could see houses or trees with his own eyes, that he ought to have faith or believe they were houses or trees, when he can clearly see that they are. That is the nature of those from the Lord's celestial kingdom, and of these angelic spirits.[47]

(3) We told them that there are few in our world endowed with interior perception, because when they are young they learn truths which they do not put into practice. A person has two faculties, called the intellect and the will. Those who only allow truths into their memory and

so a little way into the intellect, and not into their life, that is, into the will, being unable to have any enlightenment or inward sight from the Lord, say that things must be believed or one must have faith. They also reason about truths, asking whether they are true or not; in fact, they are unwilling to have them perceived by any inward sight or any kind of enlightenment through the intellect. They say this because truths for them are devoid of light from heaven, and those who see without light from heaven can see falsities as truths and truths as falsities. As a result many people in this world have become so blinded, that, even though a person does not put truths into practice, or live by them, they still say he can be saved by faith alone; as if a person's humanity did not come from and depend on the way he lives, but on knowing such things and believing them without living by them.

(4) Afterwards we talked with them about the Lord, about love directed to Him and towards the neighbour, and about regeneration. We said that loving the Lord means loving the commandments He gives, which is living according to them out of love.[48] Love towards the neighbour is wishing and consequently doing good to one's fellow citizen, one's country, one's church and the Lord's kingdom, not selfishly so as to be noticed or to earn merit, but from an affection for good.[49] On regeneration we said that those who are regenerated and put truths at once into practice in their lives, come to be able to perceive them inwardly. But those who first take truths into their memory, and then wish for and do what they demand are those who have faith; for they act from faith, which is then called conscience. The spirits said that they perceived this was so, and hence could see what faith was. I spoke with them by

means of spiritual ideas, which allow such matters to be presented and grasped lucidly.

170. These spirits with whom I had just conversed were from the northern part of their world. Then I was taken to others who were from the western part. They too wanted to investigate who I was and what sort of person, and said straight off that there was nothing but evil in me. They thought this would deter me from going any closer. I realised that they started by saying this to all comers; but I was able to reply that I was well aware of that fact, and that likewise there was nothing but evil in them, since everyone acquires evil by birth. So whatever comes from a person, spirit or angel as from his own or the self is nothing but evil, all good in anyone being from the Lord. From this they realised that I was in possession of the truth and they allowed me to talk with them.

Then they demonstrated to me their concept of evil in a person and of good in the Lord, showing how they are kept apart. They set one next to the other, so that they were almost touching, but still retaining their identity. But they were as if tied together in a way I cannot describe, so that good guided evil and restrained it from acting as it pleased; and good thus bent evil in the direction it wished, without evil being aware of it. This is how they represented the control of good over evil and at the same time a state of freedom.

(2) Then they asked how the Lord appears in the presence of angels from our world. I said that He appears in the sun as a man, surrounded by the fire of the sun, which is the source of all the light the angels in the heavens enjoy. The heat which is radiated from it is Divine good, and the light from it is Divine truth; both of these come from

Divine love, which is the fiery appearance to be seen surrounding the Lord in that sun. But that sun is only seen by
angels in heaven, not by spirits below heaven, since these
are further distanced from the reception of the good of
love and the truth of faith than the angels in the heavens
(see §40 above). The answer to their questions about the
Lord and His appearance in the presence of angels from
this world was granted to them, because it then pleased the
Lord to manifest Himself before them, and to restore to
order what had been upset by evil spirits there, about
whom they had complained. The reason why I was taken
there was to witness this.

171. Then there was to be seen a dark cloud towards the
east coming down from on high; as it descended it
changed gradually, becoming bright and taking human
form, and finally becoming a flaming beam of light surrounded by small stars of the same colour. In this way the
Lord manifested His presence with the spirits with whom I
was conversing. At His presence all the spirits there gathered together from every direction; and on their arrival the
good were separated from the wicked, the good going to
the right and the wicked to the left, and this at once as if of
their own accord. Those who went to the right were
arranged to match the quality of the good, those to the left
to match the quality of the evil among them. The good
were left to form themselves into a heavenly community,
but the wicked were thrown into hells.

(2) Afterwards I saw that flaming beam of light de-
scend quite deep into the lower parts of the earth there. It
then appeared at one time a flame colour tending to white,
at another white tending to dark, at another dark. I was
told by angels that this appearance was due to the way the

truth coming from good and the falsity coming from evil were received by the inhabitants of the lower parts of that land; it was certainly not the flaming beam which underwent these various changes. They also said that the lower parts of that land were inhabited by both good and wicked people; but they were kept well apart, in order that the wicked could be controlled by the Lord by means of the good. They added that the good are from time to time lifted up by the Lord into heaven, and their place is taken by others; this continues all the time. As the flaming beam came down the good were likewise separated from the wicked, and all was restored to order. For the wicked had by various tricks and devices penetrated into the homes of the good and attacked them. This was the reason for that visitation.

(3) The cloud, which as it came down gradually changed becoming bright and assuming human form, then becoming a flaming beam, was a community of angels with the Lord in their midst. This allowed me to know the meaning of the Lord's words about the Last Judgment reported in the Gospels, that He would come with angels in the clouds of heaven with glory and power [Matt. 24:30; Mark 13:26; Luke 21:27].

172. After this some monastic spirits were seen, some, that is, who had been travelling monks or missionaries in the world, as already mentioned above. We also saw a crowd of spirits from that world, most of them wicked ones, whom they had induced to accept their views and so seduced. These were to be seen towards the eastern regions of that world; they had driven the good away from there, and these had taken themselves off to the north side of that world, as I said before. The whole crowd together with its seducers were collected together until they numbered several thousand, and then separated, the wicked among them being cast into hells.

I was able to talk with one of the monastic spirits and enquire what he was doing there. He said it was to teach them about the Lord. Asked what else, he said about heaven and hell; and further, about trusting everything he was going to say; and further, about the power of remitting sins and opening and closing heaven. He was then tested on his knowledge of the Lord, the truths of faith, the remission of sins, personal salvation, and heaven and hell. It transpired that he knew hardly anything, having vague and false notions about every single subject. All he had was a desire to gain advantage and exercise control; this he had acquired in the world and brought with him from there. He was therefore told that, having been led by that desire to journey to that world and being so deficient in his teaching, he could do nothing for the spirits of that world but deprive them of heaven's light and substitute the darkness of hell, so ensuring that hell, and not the Lord, would rule amongst them. Moreover, he was crafty in seducing, but a fool as regards heavenly matters; and being such a one, he was then cast into hell. By this the spirits of that world were freed from these attackers.

173. Amongst other things the spirits of that world said that their visitors, the monks already mentioned, had tried their hardest to persuade them to live together in a community instead of separately and alone. For spirits and angels live and form groups in the same way as in the world. Those who lived in groups in the world, go on living in groups in the next life; those who were split up into households and families go on living separately. When these spirits had lived as people in their own world, they had been split up into groups by households, families and so clans. Consequently they were ignorant of what it was like to live together in a community. So when they were told that those visitors tried to persuade them to do this in order to rule and control them, since this was the only way they could make them their subjects and slaves, they replied that they had no idea what rule and control meant. I observed their aversion to rule and control when one of them, who accompanied us on our return journey, ran away as soon as I showed him the city where I was living, and was not seen again.

174. Then I talked with the angels accompanying me about the fact that there are two kinds of rule: one that of love towards the neighbour, the other that of self-love. The rule of love towards the neighbour is to be found amongst those who live divided into households, families and clans; the rule of self-love among those who live to-gether in a community. Among those who are divided into households, families and clans, the ruler is the father of the clan; beneath him are the fathers of families, and beneath them the fathers of each household. The father of the clan is the title given to the man who is the ancestor of the fam-ilies, and through the families of the households. But they are all ruled by love, such as a father has for his children. He teaches them how to live, does them favours and gives as much of his own to them as he can. It never occurs to him to make them his subjects or servants, but loves to have them obey him as sons do their father. Because, as is well known, this love increases as it comes down, the father of the clan acts from a more inward love than the father who is directly the progenitor of his sons. Rule in heaven is like this, since this is the kind of rule the Lord exercises; for His rule comes from His Divine love towards the whole human race.

(2) The rule of self-love, the opposite of the rule of love towards the neighbour, began when man estranged himself from the Lord. For in so far as a person fails to love and worship the Lord, so far does he love and worship himself, and he equally loves the world. Clans were then compelled in the interests of security to bring families and households together, so beginning various kinds of kingdom. In step with the growth of that love, evils of every kind increased, such as enmity, envy, hatred, revenge, brutality and trickery directed against all opponents. For nothing but evil pours forth from the self of those dominated by self-love, since a person's self is nothing but evil, so that the self, being evil, cannot receive any good from heaven. That is how it is that, when self-love is dominant, it is the father of all such evils.[50] Moreover it is characteristic of that love that, in so far as restraints are relaxed, its headlong career ends up with each individual of this sort wanting to rule over all others throughout the world, and to possess their property. In fact, not satisfied with this, he wants to rule over the whole of heaven, as may be seen by reference to the contemporary Babylon. Such now is the rule of self-love, a rule as far removed from that of love towards the neighbour as heaven is from hell.

(3) Yet however much the rule of self exhibits this character in communities, in, that is to say, kingdoms and empires, the rule of love towards the neighbour is still possible in such countries in the case of those whose faith and love for God have made them wise, since these people love the neighbour. If the Lord's Divine mercy permits, I shall describe elsewhere how these people in the heavens too

live divided into clans, families and households, even though grouped into communities, but depending upon their spiritual relationships, which arise from the good of love and the truth of faith.

175. Later I asked those spirits various questions about the world they came from, starting with questions on their worship of God and revelation. On the subject of worship they stated that clans assemble their families in one place every thirty days to listen to preaching. Then the preacher goes up into a pulpit raised a little off the ground and teaches them divine truths, which lead to goodness of life. On the subject of revelation they asserted that this takes place in the early morning when they are half-way between sleep and waking, while they are still enjoying inner light uninterrupted by bodily senses and worldly concerns. At this time they hear angels from heaven speaking about divine truths and how to live in accordance with them. When they reach full wakefulness, they see an angel dressed in white standing at their bedside, who then suddenly disappears from sight. This shows them that what they have heard is from heaven, and they can in this way tell apart a divine vision from one of another origin, for in this case the angel is not seen. They added that their preachers experience revelations in this manner, and so occasionally do others.

176. When asked about the houses they lived in, they said that these were low wooden constructions, with a flat roof surrounded by a band sloping downwards. The front part is occupied by husband and wife, the next adjacent room by the children, the rear by male and female servants. On the subject of food, they said they drank a mixture of milk and water. The milk came from cows, which had fleeces like our sheep. Asked how they lived, they said they go about naked and feel no shame at their nakedness. They restrict their contacts to those within the same family.

177. They reported that the sun of their world looks fiery to the inhabitants. Their year contains two hundred days, their day being equal to nine of our hours. They could work this out by perceiving in me the length of days in our world. They also reported that spring and summertime are for them perpetual, so that the fields blossom and the trees bear fruit all the year round. This is because their year is so short, being equivalent to only seventy-five of our days; and where years are so short the cold of winter and the heat of summer are not prolonged, so that the ground is constantly as if in spring.*

178. On the subject of engagements and marriages in their world, they related that when a daughter reaches an age to be married, she is kept at home and not allowed to go out until her wedding day. Then she is taken to a marriage parlour, where many other nubile young women have been taken, and there they are stationed behind a barrier which comes up to waist level, leaving their faces and chests exposed to view. Young men then come there to choose themselves wives. When a young man sees a girl who suits him and to whom he is mentally attracted, he takes her by the hand. If she then follows him, he takes her to a house which has previously been prepared and makes her his wife. They can tell from their faces whether their characters are suited, since each person's face is an indication of his character, with no pretence or lying. To ensure

---

*This would also be the effect if the obliquity of the axis of rotation of the planet were much less than the Earth's.—Tr.

that the whole proceeding is decorous and free from impropriety an old man is seated behind the girls, with an old woman at his side, to keep watch. There are many such places where young women are taken, and fixed times for the young men to make their choice. If they do not find a suitable girl at one place, they go off to another; and if not on that occasion, they come back at the next. They went on to say that a husband has only one wife, never more, because this would be contrary to God's order.

Author's Notes

[These notes referring to passages in ARCANA COELESTIA were in the original edition printed at the foot of the appropriate page. The references to the notes have been modernised by using figures instead of an alphabetical system. In some passages reference is made to notes previously inserted. Incorrect and doubtful references have been emended in accordance with the 3rd Latin edition of De Telluribus in Mundo nostro Solari, *ed. John Elliott (London: Swedenborg Society, 2006)]*

1 There are no spirits or angels who are not from the human race (*Arcana Coelestia* §1880).

2 The spirits of each world are in the vicinity of their world, because they come from its inhabitants and share their character. It is also so that they can be of service to them (*Arcana Coelestia* §9968).

3 The soul which lives on after death is a person's spirit, which is his real personality; in the next life it appears in a completely human form (*Arcana Coelestia* §§321, 322, 1880–1, 3633, 4622, 4735, 6054, 6605, 6626, 7021, 10594).

4 A person while still in the world is at the inner level, that is, as regards his spirit or soul, among spirits and angels of similar nature to himself (*Arcana Coelestia* §§2379, 3644, 3645, 4067, 4073, 4077).

5 A person can talk with spirits and angels; in ancient times people in our world often did so (*Arcana Coelestia* §§67–9, 784, 1634, 1636, 7802). But nowadays it is dangerous for a person to talk with them, unless he has true faith and is guided by the Lord (*Arcana Coelestia* §§784, 9438, 10751).

6 Heaven has a correspondence to the Lord, and a human being has in every detail a correspondence to heaven, so that in the Lord's eyes heaven is a man on the grand scale, and may be called the Grand Man (*Arcana Coelestia* §§2996, 2998, 3624–49, 3741–5, 4625). The whole subject of the correspondence of man and all his parts to the Grand Man who is heaven has been described from experience (*Arcana Coelestia* §§3021, 3624–49, 3741–50, 3883–96, 4039–55, 4218–28, 4318–31, 4403–21, 4523–33, 4622–33, 4652–60, 4791–4805, 4931–53, 5050–61, 5171–89, 5377–96, 5552–73, 5711–27, 10030).

7 The inhabitants of all worlds venerate the Deity in human form, that is, the Lord (*Arcana Coelestia* §§8341–47, 10159, 10736–38). They are delighted to hear that the Lord really became man (*Arcana Coelestia* §9361). It is impossible to think of God except in human form (*Arcana Coelestia* §§8705, 9359, 9972). A person can worship and love anyone of whom he has some concept, not anyone of whom he has none (*Arcana Coelestia* §§4733, 5110, 5663, 7211, 9267, 10067).

8 The Lord accepts all who are in a state of goodness and venerate the Deity in human form (*Arcana Coelestia* §§7173, 9359).

9 Spirits have access to the whole of a person's memory, but nothing passes from their memory into the person's (*Arcana Coelestia* §§2488, 5853, 6192–3, 6198–9, 6214). Angels have access to the affections and purposes which initiate and direct what a person thinks, wishes and does (*Arcana Coelestia* §§1317, 1645, 5854).

10 The spirits present with a person have control over everything in his memory (*Arcana Coelestia* 5853, 5857, 5859–60).

11 In the heavens all kinds of goodness are shared, since heavenly love shares everything of its own with others; this is the source of their wisdom and happiness (*Arcana Coelestia* §§ 549–50, 1390–1, 1399, 10130, 10723).

12 The eye corresponds to the intellect, since the intellect is the faculty of inner sight and concerned with non-material objects (*Arcana Coelestia* 2701, 4410, 4526, 9051, 10569). The sight of the left eye corresponds to truths, that is, matters of intelligence, the sight of the right eye to the kinds of good belonging to truth, that is, matters of wisdom (*Arcana Coelestia* §§4410).

13 His own life awaits each individual and accompanies him after death (*Arcana Coelestia* §§4227, 7439). The outer levels of one's life are kept closed after death, and the inner levels are opened up (*Arcana Coelestia* §§4314, 5128, 6495). At this time all the details of thought are laid bare (*Arcana Coelestia* §§4633, 5128).

14 Birds mean matters of reason and intellect, thoughts, ideas and cognitions (*Arcana Coelestia* §§ 40, 745, 776, 778, 866, 988, 991, 5149, 7441). These vary according to the genera and species of the birds (*Arcana Coelestia* §§3219).

15 Lamps together with lanterns mean truths which good makes to shine (*Arcana Coelestia* §§ 4638, 9548, 9783).

16 Lambs in heaven and in the Word mean innocence (*Arcana Coelestia* §§3994, 7840, 10132).

17 Those who make a profession of faith as the result of teaching, without living the life of faith, have no faith at all (*Arcana Coelestia* §§3865, 7766, 7778, 7790, 7950, 8094). Their inner levels are opposed to the truths of faith, though in the world they are unaware of this (*Arcana Coelestia* §§7790, 7950).

18 The Lord is the sun of heaven, the source of all light there (*Arcana Coelestia* §§1053, 3636, 3643, 4060). The Lord appears thus to those who are in His celestial kingdom, where love to Him is dominant (*Arcana Coelestia* §§1521, 1529–31, 1837, 4696). He is to be seen at middle height above the level of the right eye (*Arcana Coelestia* §§4321, 7078, 7171). The sun in the Word therefore means the Lord as regards the Divine love (*Arcana Coelestia* §§2495, 4060, 7083). The sun of the world is

not visible to spirits and angels, but its place is taken by a dark mass behind the back, opposite the sun of heaven, that is, opposite the Lord (*Arcana Coelestia* §§9755).

19 The light in heaven is strong, many times greater than the light of midday on earth (*Arcana Coelestia* §§1117, 1521–3, 1619–32, 4527, 5400, 8644). All light in the heavens comes from the Lord as the sun there (*Arcana Coelestia* §§1053, 1521, 3195, 3341, 3636, 3643, 4415, 9548, 9684, 10809). Divine truth coming forth from the Divine goodness of the Lord's Divine love is visible in the heavens as light, and provides all the light there (*Arcana Coelestia* §§3195, 3223, 3224, 5400, 8644, 9399, 9548, 9684). The light of heaven enlightens both the sight and the intellect of angels (*Arcana Coelestia* §§2776, 3138). Heaven being said to be in light and heat means in possession of wisdom and love (*Arcana Coelestia* §§3643, 9399, 9400).

20 Stars in the Word mean cognitions of good and truth, that is, truths (*Arcana Coelestia* §§2495, 2849, 4697). In the next life truths are represented by fixed stars, but falsities by wandering stars (*Arcana Coelestia* §1128).

21 Fire in the Word is love in either sense (*Arcana Coelestia* §§934, 4906, 5215). Holy and heavenly fire is Divine love, and every affection belonging to that love (*Arcana Coelestia* §§934, 6314, 6832). Hell fire is self-love and love of the world, and every lust belonging to these loves (*Arcana Coelestia* §§695, 1861, 5071, 6314, 6832, 7575, 10747). Love is the fire of life, and this is in fact the source of life itself (*Arcana Coelestia* §§ 4906, 5071, 6032).

22 Spirits and angels cannot see what is in this solar system, but they did see things through my eyes (*Arcana Coelestia* §1880).

23 The Most Ancient people in this world were able to speak using the face and lips by means of inner breathing (*Arcana Coelestia* §§607, 1118, 7361). The inhabitants of certain other

worlds have a similar manner of speaking (*Arcana Coelestia* §§4799, 7359, 8248, 10587). On the perfection and excellence of this manner of speaking (*Arcana Coelestia* §§7360, 10587, 10708).

24 A horse means what is intellectual (*Arcana Coelestia* §§2760–62, 3217, 5321, 6125, 6400, 6534, 7024, 8146, 8148). The white horse in the Book of Revelation is the understanding of the Word (*Arcana Coelestia* §§2760).

25 It is called a choir when many spirits speak in unison at once (on this see *Arcana Coelestia* §§2595–6, 3350). Their speech has a harmony (on this see *Arcana Coelestia* §§1648–9). Choirs in the next life are the means by which spirits are brought into unanimity (*Arcana Coelestia* §§5182).

26 A spiritual sphere, that of their life, flows out and pours forth from each person, spirit and angel and envelops them (*Arcana Coelestia* §§4464, 5179, 7454). Its source is their life of affection and thus thought (*Arcana Coelestia* §§2489, 4464, 6206). In the next life these spheres determine how groups are formed and also dissolved (*Arcana Coelestia* §§6206, 8630, 9606–7, 10312).

27 The Lord alone possesses merit and righteousness (*Arcana Coelestia* §§9715, 9975, 9979, 9981–2). Those who treat deeds as meritorious, those, that is, who want to earn their entrance to heaven by the good deeds they do, in the next life want to have servants and are never content (*Arcana Coelestia* §6393). They despise their neighbours and even become angry with the Lord, if they do not receive their reward (*Arcana Coelestia* §§9976). For the nature of their fate in the next life see *Arcana Coelestia* §§942, 1774, 1877, 2027. They belong to the group who appear to be sawing logs on the lower earth (*Arcana Coelestia* §§1110, 4943).

28 Chariots mean the teachings of the church (*Arcana Coelestia* §§2762, 5321, 8215). Horses mean what is intellectual (*Arcana*

Coelestia §§2760–2, 3217, 5321, 6125, 6400, 6534, 7024, 8146, 8148, 8381). The white horse in the Book of Revelation means the understanding of the Word (*Arcana Coelestia* §2760). Elijah in the representative sense means the Word (*Arcana Coelestia* §§2762, 5247). Since the Word is the source of all the church's teaching and its understanding, Elijah was called "the chariots of Israel and his horsemen"(*Arcana Coelestia* §§2762). He was therefore carried up by a chariot and horses of fire (*Arcana Coelestia* §§2762, 8029).

29 Blue tinged with red or flame colour corresponds to the good of celestial love; blue tinged with white or a shining look corresponds to the good of spiritual love (*Arcana Coelestia* §§9868, 9870).

30 The first and most ancient church in this world was a celestial church, the leading one of all (*Arcana Coelestia* §§607, 895, 920, 1121–4, 2896, 4493, 8891, 9942, 10545). A church is called celestial when its principal feature is love to the Lord, but spiritual when its principal feature is charity towards the neighbour and faith (*Arcana Coelestia* §§3691, 6435, 9468, 9680, 9683, 9780).

31 Distances in the next life appear real, and are rendered visible according to the inner states of angels and spirits (*Arcana Coelestia* §§5605, 9104, 9440, 10146).

32 Spirits and angels breathe (*Arcana Coelestia* §§3884–5, 3891, 3893).

33 People's faces in our world in ancient times were under the influence of the cerebellum; at that time faces behaved in concert with a person's inner affections. But later on the influence came from the cerebrum, when people began to lie and show in their faces pretended affections they did not feel. For the changes which their faces underwent in consequence as time went on see *Arcana Coelestia* §4325–8.

34 Contact is made between communities of spirits and angels by sending spirits to them as emissaries; these are called subordinates (*Arcana Coelestia* §§4403, 5856, 5983, 5985–9).

35 Influence is spiritual, not physical or natural, so that the spiritual world influences the natural world, but the natural does not influence the spiritual world (*Arcana Coelestia* §§3219, 5119, 5259, 5427–8, 5477, 6322). There is an apparent influence of a person's externals on his internals, but this is misleading (*Arcana Coelestia* §§3721).

36 Natural light by itself cannot yield any knowledge about the Lord, heaven and hell, how people live after death, or about Divine truths, which are a person's means of achieving spiritual and everlasting life (*Arcana Coelestia* §§8944, 10318–20). This can be established from the fact that many people, including the educated, do not believe in them, despite being born where the Word is known, and having been taught by it about these subjects (*Arcana Coelestia* §10319). It was therefore necessary for a revelation to be made from heaven, since human beings are by birth destined for heaven (*Arcana Coelestia* §1775).

37 In the next life the heathen are taught by angels, and those who have lived good lives in accordance with their own religion accept the truths of faith and acknowledge the Lord (*Arcana Coelestia* §§2049, 2595, 2598, 2600–1, 2603, 2861, 2863, 3263).

38 Angels in the heavens and people on earth understand the Word differently; the angels follow its inner or spiritual sense, people here its outer or natural sense (*Arcana Coelestia* §§1769–72, 1887, 2143, 2333, 2395, 2540–1, 2545, 2551). The Word is a unifying bond between heaven and earth (*Arcana Coelestia* §§2310, 2894, 9212, 9216, 9357, 10375). The Word was therefore written entirely by means of correspondences (*Arcana Coelestia* §§1404, 1408–9, 1540, 1619, 1659, 1709, 1783, 8615, 10687). The inmost sense of the Word deals exclusively

with the Lord and His kingdom (*Arcana Coelestia* §§1873, 2249, 2523, 7014, 9357).

39 The Word is natural in its literal sense (*Arcana Coelestia* §8783). This is because the natural is the lowest level on which the spiritual and celestial levels rest, and as it were the foundation on which the others are built. Otherwise the inner or spiritual sense of the Word, if devoid of an outer or natural sense, would be like a house without foundations (*Arcana Coelestia* §§9430, 9433, 9824, 10044, 10436).

40 The Word is the Lord as regards Divine truth, and thus Divine truth coming from the Lord (*Arcana Coelestia* §§2859, 4692, 5075, 9987). All things were created and made by means of Divine truth (*Arcana Coelestia* §§2803, 2894, 5272, 8335).

41 Motion, progress and change of place in the next life are changes in the state of inner life; they still appear as real to spirits and angels as if they were actually taking place (*Arcana Coelestia* §§1273–7, 1377, 3356, 5605, 10734).

42 After death a person keeps with him his memory of everything it contained in the world (*Arcana Coelestia* §§2475–86).

43 The light in the heavens is strong (*Arcana Coelestia* §§1117, 1521–3, 1619–32, 4527, 5400, 8644). All light in the heavens comes from the Lord, who is the sun there (*Arcana Coelestia* §§1053, 1521, 3195, 3341, 3636, 4415, 9548, 9684, 10809). Divine truth coming forth from the Lord is visible in the heavens as light (*Arcana Coelestia* §§3195, 3223, 3224, 5400, 8644, 9399, 9548, 9684). That light enlightens both the sight and the understanding of angels and spirits (*Arcana Coelestia* §§2776, 3138). The light also enlightens the understanding of people in the world (*Arcana Coelestia* §§1524, 3138, 3167, 4408, 6608, 8707, 9128, 9399, 10569).

44 A person's external sensory faculty is pictured in the spiritual world by snakes, because it is concerned with the lowest levels and as compared with a person's inner levels it lies on the

ground, and as it were, creeps. As a result those who base their reasoning on that sensory faculty were called snakes (*Arcana Coelestia* §§195–7, 6398, 6949, 10313).

45 From the Athanasian Creed.

46 Immediately after death a person rises again in spirit, and this spirit has human form and is a person in every detail (*Arcana Coelestia* §§4527, 5006, 5078, 8939, 8991, 10595, 10597, 10758). People rise again in spirit and not bodily (*Arcana Coelestia* §§10593–4). The Lord alone rose again bodily (*Arcana Coelestia* §§1729, 2083, 5078, 10825).

47 Heaven is divided into two kingdoms, one of which is called the celestial, the other the spiritual kingdom (*Arcana Coelestia* §§3887, 4138). The angels in the celestial kingdom have countless more pieces of knowledge and immeasurably more wisdom than those in the spiritual kingdom (*Arcana Coelestia* §§2718). Celestial angels do not base their thought and speech on faith as do spiritual angels, but on inner perception that this is how things are (*Arcana Coelestia* §§202, 597, 607, 784, 1121, 1384, 1385, 1442, 1919, 7680, 7877, 8780). Celestial angels only say about the truths of faith "Yes, yes" or "No, no"; but spiritual angels argue whether it is so or not (*Arcana Coelestia* §§202, 337, 2715, 3246, 4448, 9166).

48 Loving the Lord is living according to His commandments (*Arcana Coelestia* §§10143, 10153, 10310, 10578, 10645).

49 Loving the neighbour is doing good and acting justly and correctly in every task and office through affection for good, justice and right (*Arcana Coelestia* §§8120–2, 10310, 10336). Living in love toward the neighbour is living in accordance with the Lord's commandments (*Arcana Coelestia* §§3249).

50 A person's self, which he inherits from his parents, is nothing but a mass of evil (*Arcana Coelestia* §§210, 215, 731, 874–6, 987, 1047, 2307, 2308, 3518, 3701, 3812, 8480, 8550, 10283–4, 10286, 10731). A person's self is loving oneself more

than God, and the world more than heaven, and treating the neighbour as worthless as compared with oneself, except for self-ish reasons; so it is loving oneself and thus self-love and love of the world (*Arcana Coelestia* §§694, 731, 4317, 5660). Self-love and love of the world are the source of all evils, if they are dominant (*Arcana Coelestia* §§1307–8, 1321, 1594, 1691, 3413, 7255, 7376, 7488, 7489, 8318, 9335, 9348, 10038, 10742). These evils are contempt for others, enmity, hatred, revenge, brutality and trickery (*Arcana Coelestia* §§6667, 7370–4, 9348, 10038, 10742). All falsity arises from these evils (*Arcana Coelestia* §§1047, 10283–4, 10286).

List of Scripture References

1 Sam.	30:16	§108
Matt.	5:37	[§169.2]
	24:30	[§171.3]
	28:18	§91.1, [§159.3]
Luke	21:27	[§171.3]
	24:39	[§159.3]
John	1:1–4, 14, 18	§122
	5:37	§141
	10:30	§141
	14:7, 9–11	§141
	17	§66

Index of Subjects

N.B. *The numbers following each entry refer to section numbers, not to page numbers. Thus, the first reference to "Abraham" is found in §7 (coincidentally, page 7), while the second reference occurs in §158, paragraph (3), on page 119.*